ON THE JOB TRAINING
AND
WHERE TO GET IT

This book is aimed at the high school graduate who cannot go on to college. It describes his place in the laboratory, in government, in industry, and—more often than is usually supposed—in executive ranks. It shows how corporations like IBM and Bell Telephone recruit high school graduates and train them to manufacture, repair and service the most sophisticated electronic equipment. Whether the reader wants to work in a manufacturing plant, an office, in servicing or selling, or a host of other fields, here is a wealth of practical information and well-balanced advice, proving that there is challenge and a place for the high school graduate with ambition.

BOOKS BY ROBERT A. LISTON

ON THE JOB TRAINING AND WHERE TO GET IT
WHO SHALL PAY?
   Taxes and Tax Reform in America
YOUNG AMERICANS ABROAD
YOUR CAREER IN CIVIL SERVICE
YOUR CAREER IN LAW ENFORCEMENT
YOUR CAREER IN SELLING
YOUR CAREER IN TRANSPORTATION

ON THE JOB TRAINING AND WHERE TO GET IT

by R OBERT A. L ISTON

Illustrated with photographs

JULIAN MESSNER   NEW YORK

Published simultaneously in the United States and Canada by
Julian Messner, a division of Simon & Schuster, Inc.,
1 West 39 Street, New York, N.Y. 10018. All rights reserved.

Second Printing, 1974

To
Ray D. Altman, Sr.
. . . a senior citizen whose
skills belie his education

Printed in the United States of America
Library of Congress Catalog Card No. 72-11898

ISBN 0-671-32589-2 Cloth Trade
0-671-32590-6 MCE

Contents

Introduction to Second Edition

When this book was written over five years ago, many people were surprised to learn that high school graduates were being actively sought by employers in business, industry and government. The editors of the *Readers' Digest,* always searching for the new and topical, commissioned me to do an article based upon the book. It was entitled "Wanted: High School Graduates." The concept that a high school diploma, of itself, was valuable in the Twentieth Century technological America was novel. Some were even shocked by the idea. More than a few were disbelieving.

In retrospect this is not hard to understand. In 1967, the United States was enjoying a perhaps unprecedented prosperity. There was a significant shortage of engineers, scientists, teachers and other professional men and women. The college education—indeed, post-college graduate education—was touted as the key to fortune and probably fame. Without a college education, a young person was believed to be sentenced to a lifetime of dreary, probably manual work in a dead-end job, if not largely unemployed.

As we shall see, by 1973 such thinking has been heavily amended. The prosperity of the 1960s gave way to the recession of 1969-1972 with its high prices and unemployment. And the people seeking jobs included a large number

of highly trained and experienced workers in the technological, scientific and professional occupations.

To give an exaggerated example, suddenly hundreds of
thousands of teachers were unable to find jobs for which
they were trained, while plumbers in Stamford, Connecticut,
were earning $11 an hour plus 99 cents an hour vacation
pay. On a nationwide average, plumbers earned almost $8
an hour.

The lesson was not lost on large numbers of young people. By 1973, college enrollments had declined. Most colleges and universities have vacancies today where five years
ago admission standards were being raised and applicants
turned away. Clearly, large numbers of young people have
elected to skip college in favor of on-the-job training or
attendance at vocational institutes.

Writing a half decade ago, I referred so often to the need
for young people to learn a marketable skill, that it almost
became an exercise in repetition. Today I have the feeling
that there is no way to emphasize the point too much. For,
as we shall again see, the employment situation for high
school graduates is becoming competitive. Briefly stated,
college graduates are seeking jobs formerly filled by high
school graduates.

There have been many changes in the last five years, and
in this revised edition I have tried to list as many as possible.
Examples: few foresaw in 1967 that we would so quickly
have an overabundance of engineers, scientists, teachers
and other skilled occupations. It was believed then that
railroad employment would rise. It did not. Few conceived
that the commercial airline industry would do other than
continue its fantastic rate of growth. The decline in the
fortunes of the industry were simply not anticipated. Five
years ago great growth in health services was expected, but

not as much as has occurred. Few anticipated the "women's lib" movement in 1967 and the opportunities it would open for women. Similarly, the efforts to employ blacks and other disadvantaged minorities has exceeded expectations.

In this revision I have tried to chronicle as much of this as possible. Nearly every statistic in the book has been changed. The opportunities in various occupations has been thoroughly updated.

The purpose of this book is to describe training opportunities available to high school graduates. It seeks to describe the types of training offered and to reveal how you can qualify for that training.

I have tried to be as comprehensive as possible, including all of the major fields of employment where training is offered. The list includes what might be called the "traditional" opportunities, such as industrial production, building trades, retail sales and service occupations.

Particular emphasis is placed on the technical fields. Our "age" has been described in many ways—the space age, jet age, missile age—but by whatever name our times are known, they are surely the technological age. Our lives are being rapidly altered by the machines we are building, yet these very machines offer the high school graduate his greatest opportunity for training. Another purpose of this book, then, is to help you look to the future. It is only common sense in this era of fast-changing technology to learn skills that will be valuable for many years to come. The intention here is to help you visualize what those skills might be.

This is not a book for the high school dropout. He or she can read it and receive information about where to receive training. And many employers are hiring dropouts, simply because there is a shortage of high school graduates. But nothing said in this book should be construed to mean that the dropout is anything but a tragedy. The high school graduate who has made a wise choice of courses and prepared himself for training has a bright future ahead of him. The dropout faces a nearly hopeless task. He lacks the educational background sought by employers. More importantly he has provided indisputable evidence of his lack of industry, ambition and potential by failing at his first task, obtaining a high school diploma. True, he can create a better record by his job performance, but this task is at least a thousand times more difficult than it would be if he had persevered to finish high school.

There is so much training being offered to high school graduates today that it would be impossible to list it all. A book of this type can only suggest the types of training by providing a few illustrations from specific companies. To receive full value from this book, you should apply the illustrations to your situation. When you read how one company trains technicians, for example, you should realize that hundreds of companies train technicians in similar ways. As you visit the employers in your area, the personnel officers will be eager to discuss with you their specific programs for training technicians. The training opportunities exist in all fields, but it is often up to you to seek it by letting employers know that you are interested.

A number of specific companies are listed. There is absolutely no intent to endorse the company products or to suggest that the training programs are superior to those of other companies. The training programs cited are merely typical. They are illustrations of training offered by many similar firms.

I am indebted to a great many people. In particular I would like to refer to those who have provided information that went into my other career books. I have drawn upon that portion of previously obtained information which pertained to training. Gratitude is also expressed to Mrs. Nadine Simmons of the American Telephone and Telegraph Co.; Spencer Welsh, Donald Trownsell and James Fahey of the International Business Machines Corporation; A. L. "Pete" Singleton; Jerry D. Brooks; William M. Ragan, Jr., of the United States Civil Service Commission; and the Department of Labor. Particular thanks go to Mrs. Eleanor R. Seagraves of Washington, D.C.

Staff members of the Westport Public Library and my wife, Jean, who assisted in preparing the manuscript, were indispensable.

Chapter 1

Somebody Out There Wants You

Let's begin by exploding a few myths which have developed in recent years about the value of a high school education.

MYTH NO. 1—*Nobody wants to hire the high school graduate.* Nothing could be further from the truth. Research for this book indicated that there is a shortage of qualified high school graduates. Many large corporations are actively recruiting eighteen-year-olds. Competition is keen to hire them.

MYTH NO. 2—*If you haven't a college education, you can't get anything but a menial, low-paying job.* On the contrary, there are hundreds of job categories which pay high school graduates $75 to $100 a week and more—*to start.* There are several major industries in which a college education is of no particular value.

MYTH NO. 3—*Unless you have been to college, you can't get into such new "space age" industries as electronics, data processing, automation and other technical fields.* Indeed you can. Industry's big problem is finding enough qualified high school graduates.

MYTH NO. 4—*Not going to college places a low ceiling on how far you can advance.* Don't believe it. There are hundreds of thousands of managers and executives who have only a high school education. In fact, in many indus-

13

tries the high school boy or girl who learns the business "from the ground up" has an advantage over the college graduate who enters as a junior executive.

Several factors have created today's unique opportunities. A major one, certainly, is the changed character of the American economy. The technological revolution, for example, has created a tremendous demand for technicians, repairmen, installers and a great many other craftsmen that did not even exist a generation ago. In the 1940s, when your parents were teen-agers, a family had a radio, telephone, wringer-type washing machine, stove, refrigerator, toaster, mixer and a few other small appliances. Today the same home contains several transistor radios, one or more television sets, stereo, tape recorder, automatic washer and dryer, frost-free refrigerator, elaborate stove, air conditioners, complex phones that permit a person to direct-dial around the world and a dozen other appliances which are taken for granted as life's necessities. The manufacturing, installation and maintenance of these complex mechanical, electrical and electronic devices have created a tremendous need for craftsmen who are far more skilled than those of a generation past.

We are in the much publicized age of automation. Everywhere we turn we are confronted with the automatic or semiautomatic machine. They check our pulse and blood pressure, measure our brain waves, act as heart, lungs and kidneys when we are sick, measure the most infinitesimal substance of our body and permit us to reconstruct a protein molecule containing over one thousand atoms. Machines analyze the air we breathe and the earth we walk on. They forecast the weather, decode messages, permit instant worldwide communications. They issue a ticket at a turnpike toll booth or reserve a seat for us on an airplane, shine our shoes, press our clothes, provide a hot meal and fresh-brewed coffee, take our photograph, diagnose the mechanical deficiencies in our automobile—and even arrange a Saturday night date. Machines are omnipresent in our life, and therein lies a great measure of opportunity for the high school graduate. Machines are built, installed and maintained primarily by high school graduates who have been trained to do these difficult tasks.

But the technological revolution is not the only change in the American economy which has created opportunities for the high school graduate. Ours is the affluent society. Rising national wealth and higher individual earnings have created a demand for service. Americans now have leisure and the financial "wherewithal" for travel, entertainment, dining out, education and cultural enlightenment. Every middle-class American family has at least a dozen products, from foodstuffs to fuel oil, delivered to the house. We employ others to perform tasks for us which our parents did themselves a generation ago. We hire people to teach us everything from skiing to ceramics, to play athletic contests for us, beautify our hair, amuse us, make our smile attractive, keep us healthy—and perform a hundred more tasks of which we are scarcely aware.

There are now more Americans employed in providing services than in producing manufactured products. We'll take a more detailed look at what "service" means in pages to come, but at this point it should be noted that the demand for services has created millions of jobs offering great opportunity for high school graduates—who are trained to perform the service.

Our American economy has changed in that we now demand more governmental services. As Americans left the farms to become a nation almost 74 per cent urban, we discovered that the individual was able to do less for himself (or wanted to do less). We came to expect federal, state and local governments to do more for us. In such areas as housing, health, transportation, recreation, beautification, education, manufacturing—in fact, in just about every facet of our lives—we demand governmental service. As a result, government, particularly at the state and local levels, is the fastest-growing source of employment in the country.

Another factor which has created opportunity for the high school graduate is the widespread desire for a college education. Over half the high school graduates go on to college. Thus, at a time when the demand for high school graduates is increasing, there is a smaller percentage of them to fill the jobs.

Let's undertake a frank discussion of the value of a college education. Nothing that will be said in this book should be interpreted to mean that a college education is not valuable. Every person owes it to himself to obtain as much education as possible, both for personal fulfillment and for career advancement.

PERSONAL FULFILLMENT. A college education tremendously expands a person's horizons. He is exposed to knowledge about the arts, religion, social studies, science, psychology and many other subjects which are beyond the skein of his basic specialty. This makes him a more well-rounded and informed person. The four years of concentrated study and effort that goes into earning a "sheepskin" make him a more mature and disciplined person. Personal expansion is perhaps the greatest value of a college education.

But it must be said that not every person who goes to college automatically receives such personal fulfillment, nor does failure to go to college deny the high school graduate such experiences. Beginning a career after high school certainly matures and disciplines a person. The exposure to a variety of people in one's work, continued study and training expands one's horizons.

CAREER ADVANCEMENT. A college degree is absolutely essential to certain occupations: doctor, dentist, teacher, accountant, clergyman, graduate engineer, physicist, chemist, geologist, most other sciences, historian, sociologist, psychologist and many other careers. There is a trend toward requiring college education for entry into a career. A generation ago a young man was able to read for the law in the office of an attorney, but now all states require that a person have a law degree before he can be admitted to the bar. Business, industry and government increasingly recruit and train college graduates for management positions. These posts are not denied to the high school graduate, yet entering management is becoming more difficult for the person without college education.

It takes nothing away from the value of a college education, however, to say that it should not be *overvalued*. The diploma awarded at a university commencement is not an automatic ticket to fame, wealth or even employment. With the exceptions of those college graduates who have trained for specific careers in the professions, engineering or scientific fields, the collegian starts nearly on a par with the high school graduate.

This startling statement is based upon the fact that business, industry and government hire specific skills and knowledge. As an executive from a major American industrial corporation put it, "When you walk into the employment office you are a *commodity*. You have a value in terms of what you can do and what you know." This explains why industry is paying as much as $15,000 a year to hire a person who has completed graduate study in such highly technical fields as electronics and physics—and why it pays the minimum wage to someone who sweeps the floor or totes packages. If a person's college education has given him expertise in engineering and scientific skills, accounting, personnel practices, statistics, psychological testing and certain other "in demand" specialities, he will be sought after by employers and be paid a relatively high salary. But if he is a history major trying to go to work in the machine tool industry, for example, his expertise is not very much in demand. The employment manager would be far more eager to find a high school graduate who knew trigonometry or could read a blueprint.

The college graduate who has failed to prepare himself with specific, *marketable* skills and knowledge has only a slight advantage over the high school graduate who also has failed to prepare himself. The collegian is four years older and in earning the diploma has provided proof of his ambition and industriousness, but in hiring him, the employer is buying only his *potential*. The employer believes he may be able to train this person to do something useful.

The college graduate faces a peculiar problem, however. In taking his expensive and time-consuming education he must have guessed right about future career opportunities. His skill, training or knowledge must be *marketable,* and in the early 1970s, large numbers of college graduates found themselves unable to find work for which they had trained. Teachers were the most severely affected. Throughout the 1970s and beyond, the demand for teachers, especially at the elementary level, is expected to remain virtually nil. About the only openings will be for replacements of teachers who quit or die. Indeed, the employment opportunities for teachers is so tight that at least one school system is inserting a statement in its application forms that only applicants with a straight A average in college will be considered.

At this writing in 1973, job opportunities were also tight for graduate engineers and scientists, who were widely sought in the 1960s. The reversal of career opportunities was caused by cutbacks in federal spending for space exploration, defense programs and general research and development. Industry and universities also reduced their expenditures, affecting employment of engineers and scientists. As a result, large numbers of highly-skilled people are unable to find work for which they are trained—and often no work at all. The Department of Labor forecasts that the situation will improve as the decade progresses, but the opportunities for men and women with doctoral degrees is expected to remain particularly bleak.

The problem may be simply stated: there is in the 1970s an oversupply of highly trained people in some specialties. The economy cannot absorb them all. The alternative for these college graduates is to enter the job market at a lower level. They often compete for jobs with high school graduates. One young woman of my acquaintance, trained as a teacher, took a job as a bank teller—normally a position available to a high school graduate. But even this is not always possible. Employment managers will often turn away college graduates as too highly skilled for the jobs they have available. A graduate engineer, for example, who sought work as a machinery operator would probably be turned down. Employers would feel that the work was beneath him, that he would be unhappy, and would leave at the first available opportunity.

Thus, the college graduate, if he is to achieve maximum benefit from his education, must enter a field where the demand for his skills is the greatest. The Department of

Labor forecasts that in the 1970s, demand for college graduates will be greatest in the fields of computer programming (150 per cent growth), recreation (80 per cent growth), psychology (over 60 per cent growth) and social work (nearly 60 per cent growth). The entire health field also offers large opportunity.

This brief discussion of the problem of the college graduate is not a digression, for it directly affects the job opportunities for the high school graduate in the 1970s. To repeat for emphasis, some college graduates are now competing for jobs with high school graduates. In addition, the prosperity and high employment of the late 1960s has disappeared. Unemployment ranged near the 6 per cent mark from 1969 to 1972 and is not expected to return to the 4 per cent level (considered full employment) in the conceivable future. Jobs are scarce, particularly for 18-year-olds.

Some reasons for this need to be pursued. The person now in junior or senior high school follows a tremendous bulge in the population. Beginning in the late 1940s and continuing for at least a decade, the birth rate in America soared. The country had had a so-called "baby boom." In progressive years there were shortages of elementary, junior high school, high school and university facilities and teachers. These "babies," now in their twenties and thirties, are the largest single group in the population. Predictably, there is now a shortage of jobs for them.

The birth rate slowed, beginning in the 1960s, until it now approaches zero population growth. The smaller group of teenagers is now able to luxuriate in the abundance of school facilities built for the population bulge ahead of them. But a problem occurs on the job market. Today's high school graduates are finding it more difficult to find work simply because such a large group of twenty- and thirty-year-olds have flooded the job market at a time when the economy is depressed. Employers will often choose an older, more mature person for an available job over an eighteen-year-old high school graduate.

Another factor affecting jobs is the large cutback in the numbers of young men drafted by the military services. There are several hundred thousand young men looking for jobs today who were not in the job market five years ago.

The job market for high school graduates is simply more competitive today. Yet, the fact remains that if the eighteen-year-old has a marketable skill, he will be sought after and employed at a higher salary than those who can offer only potential. *It cannot possibly be emphasized enough that if you are not going to college, you must prepare yourself by developing a specific, marketable skill.* When you do that, you have one foot up the ladder already.

To avoid the specific and make general statements is to invite the inaccurate, but with truthfulness it can be said there is a significant difference in the roles of the college trained and the high school graduate. Employers seek *knowledge* from a college graduate, while demanding more *skill* from the high school student. They want, in the college trained, a person who has information learned from books, while in the high school graduate they look for a person who can *do* things. There are many exceptions, but in general the college person tends to design an object, and a high schooler to build and repair it. The collegian tends to draft an idea or proposal, the eighteen-year-old to reproduce and disseminate it. Conception is the collegian's forte, performance the high schooler's.

But do not misconstrue this statement to mean that the person who has more education will always "boss" the high schooler. In truth, it works out this way a significant portion of the time, but not always. Ours is a pragmatic society, predicated entirely on results. The person who can "do things," who has a record of performance, receives the greatest rewards. The engineer may design an excellent machine, but it is useless unless the technician and production worker are able to operate it efficiently. The fellow who learns from having performed a task with his hands develops a knowledge and understanding which the person who knows only theory can envy. The individual who can perform and then learn theory is the most sought-after individual in our society, whether in a factory, office or store.

What is being said here is that the college-educated and the high school graduate have different functions and unique roles in our economy. Each is valuable and each has a place. We can't have all designers and no builders. We can't all be theoreticians and none of us performers. The thoughtful young person ought to consider himself, his abilities and his ambitions carefully and then decide whether to begin his career after high school. And if he decides not to go to college, the world is just as much his oyster as it is for his buddy who enrolled in the university.

A major premise of this book is that there are no menial jobs, only menial people. The person who takes a job stacking cans in a supermarket can do that the rest of his life, or he can be launching a career which will carry him to the highest levels of supermarket management. A fellow can be a waiter all his life, or he can start at the bottom to learn hotel and resort management. A girl can be a file clerk forever, or she can begin to learn filing techniques as an avenue toward a career as an administrator or expert in office management.

There is nothing wrong with being a can stacker, waiter, file clerk or any other expert in simple tasks, if that is what you want. The world needs such people. What is being said here is that the fact you have *only* a high school education does not preclude you from rising higher or performing more complex and valuable tasks. As has been said, there is only a relative handful of professional and scientific careers that are closed to you unless you go to college.

Those of you going to work after high school ought to be mentally prepared to manage your career somewhat differently than the college graduate does. This may be the single most important point made in this book. It needs to be emphasized, because teachers and guidance counselors are sometimes unaware of it since they have a college-oriented background. After you discuss career problems with industrial personnel officers and with executives who have gone into management from the ranks, the problems faced by the high school graduate become evident.

His first task is to learn to *do* something either in school or as soon as possible afterward. It is important that you decide early what you want to do and set about learning to do it. There are significant exceptions, but the public high schools as now constituted offer only limited opportunities to learn a marketable skill.

One of the exceptions is for commercial students. Hundreds of thousands of high school students, predominantly girls, learn typing, shorthand, filing, business machine operation and similar clerical tasks. They leave high school with marketable skills that are much in demand.

Graduates of vocational high schools are another exception. They have learned such marketable skills as beauty operators, automobile and other types of mechanics, machinists, carpenters, electricians and other building craftsmen, printing tradesmen and perhaps a half hundred other fields. The commercial and vocational graduates have something to offer when they open the door of the employment office. They are already well ahead in the occupational game.

It is the rest of the high school graduates who pose the problem: the academic student who prepares for college and then does not go, and the person who receives what is customarily called a *general diploma*. In the last half dozen years, particularly since the full effect of the technological revolution began to be felt, business and industry has become aware that a significant percentage of high school graduates who intend to go to work are not prepared for jobs in business and industry. In short, they lack marketable skills.

Henry M. Boardman, manager of community relations at the Western Electric plant in Kearny, New Jersey, is actively engaged in a pioneer program in the Newark area to help public school administrators make the curriculum more practical. He gave an example of what he means by practical: "If you take a metal bar six feet long, how many two-inch pieces can you cut from it?" Now this is a practical problem, for there are many times in industry when a workman is expected to requisition a quantity of materials to be divided into smaller lots. As Mr. Boardman put it, "If the teacher says to him that he can get thirty-six two-inch pieces out of a six-foot bar, he is wrong. You must leave an allowance for the size of the blade that does the cutting." Another example given by Mr. Boardman: normally trigonometry is a subject taught in the academic and technical courses, but a person who becomes a machinist or tool and die maker has to know some "trig"—not all phases of it, but he has to become an expert in right angle trigonometry.

In order to assist high schools in offering the sort of practical knowledge needed by industry, Western Electric has prepared and offers a series of courses in applied mathematics. This is math not for the person going on to college, but for the high school graduate launching a career in industry. The following are a few examples of the types of problems the students learn to solve in these courses:

- A detail is 1⅜ inches long, how much 1½-inch material will be required to cut out 176 pieces? That is a problem in multiplication of fractions.
- What is the diameter of the shaft required to mill a 1.375-inch square? That is a problem in plane-surface measurements.
- To drill 13 holes equally spaced on the circumference of a circle that has a 4-inch diameter, what is the chord and the radius?
- If 14 men can make 36,000 details in one hour, how many details can they make in three hours and 40 minutes? A problem in proportion.

The need to make high school curricula more career oriented has been recognized by educators in the last five years. A million more students are enrolled in vocational courses. Yet a great deal more needs to be done to equip the non-college-bound graduate with the necessary knowledge and practical skills to enable him or her to compete successfully in the job market. The U.S. Office of Education, which administers federal funds, has begun programs to augment career preparation in high schools.

The message here is that if you are preparing to enter industry, do everything you can to learn practical information about mathematics, electrical theory, basic electronics, mechanics and whatever would be appropriate and useful to the field in which you want to work. Learn a marketable skill in any way you can—in school courses, by reading a book, taking a special night course or correspondence course. Use your part-time job to build a future. If you want to be a machinist, get a job sweeping floors in a machine shop. If you want to build a career in merchandising, try part-time clerking in a store. Do something related to your future occupation, if only to learn the special terminology. Use your hobbies to build a skill. Tinkering with the engine in the family car has fostered many an automobile mechanic. Flying model planes, home sewing, preparing microscopic slides and endless other hobbies have helped a person develop a marketable skill.

The effort you invest in learning a marketable skill indicates a cardinal difference between the career development of a high school graduate and the college graduate. The college graduate entering a profession tends to have a career which develops vertically. A teacher, for example, tends to be promoted to assistant principal, principal, some form of supervisor, assistant superintendent and superintendent. The promotional opportunities are fairly well defined. Sometimes this is true for the high school graduate. The retail clerk tends to be promoted to sales positions of greater difficulty, to supervisor, sales manager and merchandise manager. But in many careers, there is not an orderly path of promotion. There is no precise way, for example, that a person can go from unskilled factory worker into management—yet many have done it. When you examine the careers of men who have made the leap from unskilled laborer to executive, you discover each was someone unique. The individual moved laterally sometimes, instead of vertically, leapfrogging into another area of the business which afforded him his opportunity.

The common denominator of the men who began at the bottom of the industrial ladder and rose to the top was that they did not remain unskilled for long. They worked and studied, enrolled in company training courses, and augmented them with night courses. They may not have had a college education when they started, but they earned a diploma or its equivalent within a few years. In brief, if they started without a marketable skill, they soon learned one, for they realized that what they made of themselves was entirely up to them.

The challenge to the high school graduate is that he starts at or near the bottom of whatever line of endeavor he enters. The privilege is that he can learn and progress. The challenge is that he may be lost in a large group of people who lack ability, determination or ambition to rise above the lower employment levels. The career-minded 18-year-old must find a way to stand out by his ability, his desire to learn and his willingness to accept responsibility. One of his obstacles, to be frank, is the union seniority system, which assures that the oldest men of ability are the first to be promoted. In large companies seniority tends to thwart the ambition of younger men far down in the seniority lists. But there are ways around the seniority system, as will be discussed in a later chapter.

Being a stand-out from the crowd at the bottom is not very difficult. Most personnel officers, both in interviews and in pre-employment testing, look for the individual with leadership qualities and ambition. They want to hire young men and women who are potential supervisors and executives.

You can have a career if you are untrained. Business and industry, as well as government, offer thousands of different training programs for the unskilled high school graduate. These programs, plus those which you can initiate for yourself, enable the high school graduate to take full advantage of the unparalleled opportunities which lie before him today. This book, then, is about those opportunities for training.

Chapter 2

Training in the
Technological Industry

Industrial personnel officers emphasize that the young person seeking employment today should look to his future, specifically his technological future. He should not train to make buggy whips at the dawn of the automotive era.

There are a number of products on a par with buggy whips today. Who would have guessed only a few years ago that nylon would replace silk in hosiery, that the fountain pen would lose its popularity to the ball point, that radio tubes would all but disappear, that plastic would replace a wide variety of metal, leather, wood and fabric products. Looking to the future, a farsighted person could wonder if paper clothes will remain just a novelty. Will the auto mechanic of the future be required to know a great deal of chemistry because cars will be powered by electricity rather than by the internal combustion engine? Will metals popular today be replaced by lighter, stronger metals and plastics unheard of today? Will the water a person drinks in the future be fresh, or will it be reprocessed for use again and again? Will foods all be natural, or will Americans be dining on synthetic edibles? How many jobs done by human labor today will be performed by machines in decades hence?

The young person launching his career today must

consider not only how marketable his skill is likely to be in twenty or forty years, but whether the products he makes with his skill will even exist at that future date. The effect of technology on skill development shows in the report by the United States Department of Labor that "technician" is perhaps the fastest-growing occupational group. Everybody talks about the technician, but no one can define him. The word covers a large, amorphous group of skills that are much in demand in the technological industries. There are electro-mechanical technicians, computer technicians; electrical technicians; mechanical, chemical, air-conditioning, refrigeration and heating technicians; metallurgical technicians; vacuum technicians; and scores more. Just about anybody who possesses the skills to perform tasks based on scientific knowledge is a technician.

Does the high school graduate have a career in the technological industries? Indeed he does. Thousands of firms are actively recruiting high school graduates whom they can train to manufacture, install and repair the new, exotic, "space age" products.

To obtain a firsthand look at these new careers, I journeyed to East Fishkill, New York, where the International Business Machine Corporation maintains a huge plant to manufacture computer components.

At East Fishkill it is possible to see a clear division of the skills needed in today's and tomorrow's technology. The people who designed the components were scientists. The men who designed the equipment which manufacture it were engineers. Technicians build and maintain this machinery. The men and women who operate the equipment are high school graduates—and they are learning skills invaluable to them for decades to come.

It is impossible for any writer to accurately portray the

wide variety of careers for the high school graduate in technological industries. All that can be done is to provide a few illustrations of available careers. If you are interested in working in the technological industries—and you should be—you will have to apply the illustrations to your particular interests and situations. The requirements of the jobs will vary, as will the tasks performed and the working conditions. But by looking at one plant which is typical, it is possible to gain insights into what to expect at many other plants making many different technological products. With this in mind, let's see what is involved in your getting a job at IBM's East Fishkill plant.

You begin by going to the employment office at the plant, where you are asked to fill out an application. It is important in filling out any employment application that you give as much information as possible about yourself, your family background, your educational courses, hobbies, part-time jobs and anything else that is asked on the form. Complete answers to questions not only provide the interviewer with much information about you but also form a basis for your future career advancement. In most large corporations, personnel records are highly systematized. In the case of IBM, as with many other companies, information about you is fed into a computer. At some time in the future, when the company is seeking to promote employees, it may ask the computer for a list of people who are of a certain age and have similar backgrounds, education, experience and other qualities. The facts which you put on your application months or years before may well come to the fore as the computer does its work.

After you have filled out an application, you are interviewed again. This is one of the most important steps in your getting the job. If you look at yourself as the company does for a moment, you will soon see why. The company doesn't really expect you to know anything about transistor chips, solid-logic modules or computers. It asks that you have the aptitude, interest and potential to learn. If you have that potential, it is willing to invest a good bit of time, effort and expense in teaching you whatever will make you useful. The personnel interviewer's task is to decide whether you have the potential.

Toward this end, he will discuss anything on that application which may enable him to judge the person you not only are today but are likely to become in the future. He will ask you about your high school courses. Which ones did you like? Which ones did you do well in and why? He'll want to know why you aren't going to college, why you want to work in the electronics industry, why you are interested in IBM and why this particular plant. He may ask why you didn't apply at another electronics plant in the area. All of these questions are a means of judging your interest and motivation. There are no pat answers to these questions— other than truthful ones.

There are many answers to these questions. One applicant may say that he wants to work at the plant because several of his friends are employed there, and this would be a perfectly acceptable answer. For another applicant with a different circumstance, the answer will seem less valid.

Wherever you are applying, it is a good idea to have investigated the company. Be familiar with its reputation and its products. Try to know something of the type of work performed there and the tasks you will be expected to do. How do you learn? From books such as this, by talking to employees and by reading company literature, which is available for the asking. Every company looks askance at the applicant who walks in looking for just any old job, ignorant of what he is seeking. Company pride—and simple common sense—tells them that the best employee will be the man or woman who truly wants to work for them.

In addition to your interest and motivation, the interviewer is judging your character. Do you have a cooperative attitude? Will you fit in? Will you accept instruction readily? Do you have leadership qualities? Will carrying responsibility come easily to you?

If you make a favorable impression during your interview, you will be asked to take some tests. These will measure your general ability and especially your aptitude for work in the electronics industry—or whatever field you are entering. You may already know your aptitudes, but then you may be surprised. I was amazed at one time to discover that I had a modicum of mechanical aptitude after growing up to believe I had none.

You should try to do as well as you can on these tests. They help to determine whether you have the basic abilities which will enable you to learn the needed skills. Test scores are evaluated in various ways by different companies. At IBM, for example, your test scores are compared with ratings of company employees presently doing the job you will fill. In all companies, there are low scores which may eliminate you as an applicant. For all those who score above the minimum, some judgment is used by the personnel officer. If, for example, you make a very favorable impression during your interview but score only moderately on your aptitude tests, he might still be inclined to hire you. If you score high in aptitude but make a poor impression during the interview, he still might hire you—and then again he might not.

It is important to remember when you are applying for

a job—any job—that you are being considered for a specific position. No companies hire employees just to have them around. They have specific positions to be filled, and they are looking for the best available applicants. So the interviewer will discuss with you the job or jobs he has available and for which he feels you may be qualified. He will describe it to you, so that you have a full understanding of what is demanded of you, what you will learn and the promotional opportunities available. You owe it to yourself, and you will be helping to make a favorable impression, if you ask questions until you have that understanding.

In most companies the personnel officer decides whether to hire you, but only after he has checked the accuracy of your application. He will seek information about your high school performance and check with the individuals you have named as references. Since your school performance is the best evidence of the type of person you are, giving a teacher or guidance counselor as a reference is a good idea. If you have had part-time employment, a previous employer makes a good reference. The investigator may check on your character, credit or criminal record, if it is appropriate. You will also be given a physical examination to determine if there is any reason you cannot physically fulfill the tasks you will be asked to do.

In IBM and other companies the personnel manager does not make the final decision on whether to hire you. You are interviewed by the manager of the department in which you will work. He will show you around the department and explain the job you will do. He wants to judge whether you will be able to learn the job and whether you will fit in with the men and women working under him. If he decides you are the best applicant for the job, you are hired.

At IBM and many other companies you are hired on your

potential to learn; but if you have a particular background, you are more likely to be hired. At East Fishkill, Mr. Thomas Soules, assistant to the general manager, said it would be "very desirable" if you had a couple of years of mathematics such as algebra and trigonometry and "very desirable" if you had courses in physics and chemistry. Good grades in these courses indicate your interest and aptitude for the technical field. If you wish to prepare especially for careers in technology you can read a book or two on the subject and perhaps take an extension or reputable correspondence course which would give you an understanding of basic electronics. You might work part time in a store or factory which deals with electrical or electronic equipment. In short, anything you can do which enhances your knowledge of the field in which you want to work is a "plus" which may lead to your employment, for companies know that knowledge and experience will help you to progress faster in your training. Ideal preparation would be to join a cooperative program such as IBM offers for seniors in the area of its East Fishkill plant. As part of their studies, seniors work at the plant, gaining considerable familiarity with electronics. But Mr. Soules emphasizes that all of these extra preparations are secondary, unless you have made a good record in high school. Extension courses and part-time work will never substitute for regular homework.

Most untrained high school graduates begin at the East Fishkill plant by learning to operate production machinery. This equipment is highly complex, but IBM engineers have perfected its operation until it is relatively simple. The machinery performs one step in the process of making computer components. On the simplest machinery, the operator sets the equipment to do its job, feeds materials into it and runs tests to determine if the machinery is performing correctly. Yet there is room for error, and an operator can ruin a great deal of expensive work if he is careless.

IBM trains high school graduates to be operators in one to three weeks. For the simplest machines, this training is done on the job. The departmental manager or technician works with the trainee, explaining how the equipment works and the tasks the operator is to perform. Under supervision, the operator begins to work the equipment himself. As his ability and reliability increase, the amount of supervision he requires gradually lessens, although he continues to receive some supervision as long as he remains with the company.

What is expected of you during your training phase? If you put yourself in the position of the company executives, the answer is easy. IBM wishes to make a complex product with a high degree of reliability. It has installed automatic apparatus which makes scores of tests upon computer components so that any faulty ones are rejected. Furthermore, it has made a great investment in the machines and production lines which manufacture its miniature components. It desires, therefore, to protect both the product and the manufacturing equipment. Company executives know when you are hired that you don't know a thing about making computer components. They endeavor to teach you everything you need to know to perform a particular job, but even the best instructors cannot be certain that you fully understand. Therefore, you have a responsibility to understand what you are doing and to ask questions until you do. At any time when you are "stuck" and don't know what to do next, you are expected to seek help. Ignorance is not bliss in the technological industry. The person who goes blindly ahead and makes a mistake will be criticized, while the individual who asks a question to avoid making a mistake will be commended.

All IBM employees, as in other companies, are evaluated regularly on their performance. The immediate supervisor, in your case the departmental manager, rates your work as outstanding, exceeds requirements, meets requirements, meets minimum requirements or inadequate. Mostly the rating is based on your job performance, both the quantity and quality of production. You may run a great many pieces through your equipment, for example, but if many of them were rejects, your performance will hardly qualify as outstanding. Other factors, such as your attitude, cooperativeness and leadership, are considered in your rating. Each time you are rated, the manager discusses your rating with you, showing you how you might improve. Good ratings naturally play an important role in your eventual promotion.

The technological industries place a high value on knowledge and skills, so throughout your employment you will have many opportunities to improve both. The East Fishkill plant, for example, offers voluntary education courses. There are more than fifty courses which company employees can attend free of charge on their own time. There are classes in IBM systems programming, electricity and electronics, mathematics, secretarial subjects, blueprint reading, mechanical drawing, machine shop practices and general subjects such as speech, report writing and reading improvement. Taking these courses is no guarantee of a promotion, but they enhance your knowledge and performance.

There are many other opportunities for advancement and skill development for the high school graduate. After you have become proficient in your beginning level job, you will be assigned to more complex and challenging operations. You will be trained anew, partly on the job as before, but now there may be some classroom instruction. As your ability and confidence increase, you may be permitted to do some preventive and other types of maintenance work on the equipment itself. This is one of the steps toward becoming a technician.

"Technician," as we know, is a loosely used word to denote skilled individuals in technological industries. They perform a wide variety of tasks dealing with both equipment and processes, tasks that require more knowledge than a production worker would have, yet are not as demanding as that done by graduate engineers.

At the East Fishkill plant there are at least three types of technicians. Some have had two years of training at a bona fide electronic technician's school. Others have had special courses, while a third type has risen from the ranks of operators. Called departmental technicians, the latter assist the manager both in supervision and in solving the technical problems that arise in his department. Departmental technicians may be trained in a 64-week course consisting of classroom, laboratory and on-the-job study. It is a rigorous course, endeavoring to give the student thorough knowledge of electronics, math, physics, mechanics, chemistry and a half dozen other subjects that he will need to fully understand the manufacturing processes and the equipment.

Operators are selected for this most valuable training on the basis of their performance, interest and potential. You may apply for the training, but your manager must also recommend you as a person he believes capable of becoming a technician. You are then interviewed and tested before enrollment. If you pass the course and become a technician, you have learned skills marketable throughout your life.

There is another training program open to operators who qualify. It is a thirty-nine-month course—almost as long as a college education—which trains manufacturing technicians to repair and maintain IBM production equipment. The student in this course learns a bewildering variety of valuable skills, including mechanics, electronics, vacuum technology, physics, chemistry, how to handle gases, heating, cooling, tool and die making and several others. All of these specialties are used in the maintenance of the complex IBM manufacturing equipment. This equipment is so new and so special that no ordinary plumber or electrician would know how to repair it. The company trains its own men as specialists on its own equipment. The men they train are as able craftsmen as may be found anywhere.

If we examine the East Fishkill operation more closely, we can see there is ample opportunity for advancement. An able operator may become a departmental technician, from whose ranks departmental managers are usually chosen. Edward O'Donnell, one of the East Fishkill managers, went from operator to technician to manager in just four years, although he is perhaps not typical. Above the manager are project managers, who supervise several departments. The next steps are to superintendent and to program manager. The latter at East Fishkill might be in charge of production of transistor chips, for example.

How far can a person with a high school education go in a technological industry such as IBM? Some men have become general managers, corporate vice-presidents and other top officers. But it is only fair to say that they are exceptions. In technology, most top management positions go to the men who have a scientific and engineering education. But a high school graduate who learns the business with his hands, takes advantage of all available training, goes to night school and demonstrates great skill in his performance and fine qualities of leadership could reasonably aspire to become a superintendent. But any such discussion must certainly be prefaced with this remark: It depends on you, the type of person you are, your ambition, your motivation. Believe it, there are still Horatio Algers in this land.

The technological industries, like others, permit, indeed encourage, high school graduates to improve themselves by moving laterally. A lateral movement is one that perhaps does not involve a promotion, but simply transfers you to a line of work which you may like better or feel is more promising for you. For example, an operator could transfer to the stock room. Here he could develop a career path as a production expeditor, analyzer of parts and on up into production control. Another lateral move would be into computer operation, if you showed the aptitude. This, in turn, could lead to computer programming. Other moves could be into personnel or administrative services.

Many of you taking a job after high school will want to consider such lateral transfers. It is a lucky man who discovers the work he likes in his first effort. After some time in a job, you may discover that your skills in your particular job do not keep pace with your ambition.

IBM is a giant company in the electronics field. The opportunities for training and advancement which it offers are both typical and progressive for the industry. But whether it is a giant corporation or a tiny shop manufacturing electronic components, you can have a career in electronics with a high school education. The skills you will learn will be marketable throughout your life.

Chapter 3

More Opportunities for
Technical Training

Thousands of companies train high school graduates to perform modern technical skills, then retrain them to perform still newer tasks. Every technological industry you can think of—from chemicals to metals, aircraft and rockets to highways and building construction, instrumentation to air conditioning—train its own skilled workmen, for employers realize that with very few exceptions no one is going to train them for them. The vocational high schools and private colleges and technical schools cannot supply the quantity of skilled labor needed.

For the most part, a particular industry trains its men and women to fit its particular needs. They learn to operate, install or maintain the equipment used by the company. But the skills learned are highly marketable. They make the person most valuable to the company which taught him, and if he leaves the firm for any reason, he can "sell" his skills to other companies in the same industry and even in other industries.

To illustrate technical training offered by industry which leads to marketable skills, let's examine the telephone industry. There are hundreds of small and large phone companies, but the twenty-three firms which make up the Bell

Telephone System of the American Telephone and Telegraph Company provide about eighty-four per cent of the telephone service in the United States.

The term "telephone company" is a misnomer, for Bell companies are in truth communications companies. Their activities include teletypewriter communications, wirephoto, mobile radio such as you might have in your car, television and radio transmission, communications satellites such as Telstar, Data-Phone processes by which business equipment and computers are linked nationwide and microwave transmission. "Telephone equipment" involves the latest in electronics, electromechanics, radio, television, automation and other technologies. Despite the technological demands of the industry, Bell System telephone companies train thousands of high school graduates annually to manufacture, install and maintain this equipment. It takes young men and women who, as Gene Nagel, an AT&T executive puts it, "wouldn't know a volt from a watt" and trains them to a high level of expertise.

The amount of training provided telephone employees is staggering. During a recent three-month period, Bell System companies provided 1,839,845 hours of classroom instruction for plant employees. This training was given to 224,000 of the approximately 280,000 plant employees during this period. The formal training does not include on-the-job training, nor does it include any of the training given to traffic employees (such as operators), who operate telephone equipment, or to commercial employees, who provide sales, billing and related services. The nearly 1,900,000 hours of off-the-job training was provided in just three months for plant employees who install and maintain telephone equipment.

The importance telephone companies place upon skill development shows in the fact ninety-eight per cent of all

Bell Company "first line" managers do not have a college education. One out of every three middle- and upper-management executives have come up through the ranks with less than a college education. Thus, the high school graduate has unlimited opportunity in the telephone industry both for training and for advancement into management. He is measured more by what he can do than by the length of his education.

Everyone uses the telephone. There are about ninety-five million telephones in the United States. They are so omnipresent, operate so consistently and require so little effort by the user that we sometimes fail to realize what a complex system is involved.

If there were only a few phones, it would be simple to run a wire from one home to another, but with ninety-five million telephones, switching of immense complexity is necessary. When you pick up the telephone handpiece, a switch inside the telephone closes and current flows through the telephone from the central office. There, a relay switch closes, putting your telephone in the circuit with the equipment that will put your call through. The dial tone tells you the circuit is closed and the equipment is now ready for your call.

What is a switch and relay? A switch, as you know, is two electrical contacts so arranged that they can be brought together by manual or mechanical means. Your doorbell is a manual switch. When you press the button, it closes the circuit and allows the bell to ring. In a telephone switch, an electromagnet does the work of your finger. When you turn the current to the electromagnet on and off, the magnet opens or closes the switch. In the telephone system, electromagnets make parts rotate, move up and down, pivot, tilt and perform other essential tasks of circuitry. Combinations of electromagnets and switch contacts are called relays, and millions of them make a telephone system. A modern dial office serving 10,000 lines will have about 70,000 relays.

When you dial a number on your phone—the number 5, for example—it interrupts the circuit five times. Each interruption in the circuit causes a relay in the central office to repeat the electrical pulse—a group of five pulses when you dial five, three pulses when you dial three, and so on. When the pulse reaches the central office, they set more relays into operation. Each relay closes another connection, extending the electrical circuit a little further. But in what direction? The first three numbers you dial identify the central office of the telephone you wish to call. The last four digits identify the circuitry (by closing relays) which leads to the specific telephone you wish to contact.

All of this is basic, compounded by the sheer volume of circuits and calls being made. Then there are the complexities. By dialing 10 digits, you can extend the circuitry to any telephone in the United States. It becomes further complicated with push-button or Touch Tone service. When you push a button instead of rotating a dial, sound tones are translated into electrical pulses which activate the relays that control the circuits. Then there are crossbar switches, which are already replacing the old step-by-step switching systems described. This system permits as many as 10 simultaneous connections to be made by just one switch. Then there is electronic switching (EES), using transistor chips and other miniature devices. EES is more rapid, convenient and flexible. You need dial only two to four digits on frequently called numbers. You can set up your own conference call by dialing four persons in turn and add a third person to a conversation already in progress. You can have calls transferred automatically to another number while you are away from home—and there are many other conveniences. EES is only beginning to be installed at this writing.

This brief discussion of telephone techniques is intended to show the complexity of modern telephone service. Rather than scaring you with its complexity, it should encourage you, because telephone companies take young men who wouldn't know that volt from a watt and train them to install and repair this electrical, mechanical and electronic equipment.

There are seven major categories of telephone plant employees: 92,000 central office craftsmen, 22,000 central office installers and 102,000 telephone and switchboard installers. Among the specialties: a lineman places poles, cables, open wire and underground cable out of doors. A frameman hooks cable to the central office switching equipment. The splicer splices cable, which is simply a collection of individual wires encased for ease of handling. The central office repairman maintains central office equipment. The installer places telephone and switchboard equipment in the homes and offices of subscribers. The repairman fixes subscribers' equipment which has broken down. The installer-repairman performs both of the latter jobs.

When you are employed by the telephone company, following interviews, aptitude testing, reference checks and physical examination, chances are you will begin as either a lineman or a frameman, or in telephone parlance an "outside man" or "inside man." There is no particular rigidity to these entry-level jobs. A person can transfer between inside and outside jobs as his training progresses.

Mr. Nagel emphasizes that the initial training format may vary depending on the locale, the need for workmen and the abilities of the individual. In general, an inexperienced lineman will receive a week or two of rather formalized training. He will learn the use of his tools and how to climb a pole safely. The latter is usually done slowly. The new man climbs only a couple of feet at first, reaching the top of a twenty-foot pole only as he has gained confidence and experience with his safety equipment. He will also become familiar with the heavy equipment carried on the trucks. This includes hole digging equipment and various kinds of hydraulic gear.

Throughout his training, the greatest possible emphasis is placed on safety. The lineman is outfitted with a belt and special spikes to ensure his safety while climbing. Hydraulic chair lifts are used to eliminate some of the climbing. It should be noted that, unlike some power company linemen, the telephone man does not work with high-voltage lines. Telephones customarily operate on low power.

After his orientation and familiarization, the trainee will work beside an experienced employee who helps him both with his performance and with his safety. Normally two or three men work as a unit on a truck.

The frameman usually receives all his initial training on the job, learning under supervision of experienced employees. Another entry-level job is that of the cable splicer helper, who assists experienced men while learning the intricate splicing tasks.

Some men remain linemen and framemen during their entire careers with the phone company because they either like the work or fail to progress to more demanding assignments. Ordinarily both linemen and framemen progress to either installer or installer-repairman. The former is the person who runs the wire from the pole into the house and installs the phone in the house, along with extension phones, jacks and other equipment desired by the subscriber. Normal progressions are to installation of more complex switchboard equipment and to repair of subscriber equipment, as well as installation of it.

Telephone companies market a wide variety of telephone equipment today, from the familiar dial or push-button phone to those which handle several lines and permit switching to various extensions. Both installers and repairmen tend to progress from simpler to more complex equipment in accordance with their ability and experience. Their training occurs both on the job and in formal classroom settings.

Another normal progression is to the high-level skills such as repairmen and central office repairmen. Again there are various levels of competence. Central office repairmen can become experts in some of the most complex electronic equipment manufactured today. But these expert technicians began their careers as linemen and framemen. Experience, aptitude and many hours of classroom instruction turned them from men who didn't know a volt from a watt into electronic technicians possessing a highly marketable skill.

There are many avenues for expertise. A person can specialize in teletypewriter or telephoto equipment, radio and television transmission and several other categories. The men who installed and today maintain the equipment for receiving signals via the Telstar satellite, which links the world by instant voice and picture communication, were company-trained telephone craftsmen. It is no exaggeration to say that few businesses offer the high school graduate such abundant opportunities to learn marketable skills as America's telephone industry.

Just a cursory glance at some of the training courses reveals the extent of the expertise learned by Bell telephone employees: circuit reading; electronic switching; automatic operator training equipment; large-system control terminal for mobile telephone system; DATASPEED Tape-to-Tape System; Defensive driving; working aloft (safety); Touch Tone calling; recording and summarizing reports; customer service repair; personal signaling system; basic electricity; central office power plant maintenance; basic refrigeration, farm interphone systems; manhole atmosphere testing for gases; air conditioning; microwave radio relay; television operating center; radio license preparation; cathode ray oscilloscope; telegraph principles and application; transistors and a great many others too complicated to list here.

These training classes use the latest teaching methods, including programmed learning, in which the student goes at his own pace, and video-taping, which enables employees to observe classroom instruction while still on their jobs. Students use manuals which set forth all phases of telephone operation, and in many cases the actual equipment on which they will be working. Thus, in addition to lectures, demonstrations and other formal classroom methods, students participate in "lab" work, actually performing the work they have just read or heard about. If the equipment is too bulky to be brought to the training centers, as in the case of central office equipment, the students go out into the field to learn on the equipment first hand.

It is said in the Bell companies that training never stops. No man ever knows enough, so rapidly does the technology change. We have already discussed the electronic switching system. By 1975 nearly thirty per cent of the telephones will be served by such equipment. Communications satellites will be used extensively in long distance dialing. By 1975 half of all overseas calls will go through satellites. Traffic service positions (TSP) will replace the cord switchboard used for handling person-to-person and collect calls. This equipment will reduce the operator worktime per call by about thirty per cent. Automatic intercepting may reduce the number of calls requiring operators' assistance. Semiautomatic information service will enable an operator to provide a requested telephone number using an electronic processor instead of a telephone directory. And there are many other developments in telephone equipment which will ensure that training goes on forever.

The most advanced skills may be learned by the person who has the interest and the aptitude, but an employee may also move vertically into management. He may learn only to be an expert lineman, for example, but be promoted to supervisory positions over other linemen. Or he may move into management positions after becoming an installer or repairman or after gaining any other skill.

The normal career path is to foreman (of a lineman crew, installation crew, or whatever); second-level supervisor; district plant superintendent, who would supervise 150 to 200 employees; division plant superintendent (over 1,500 to 2,000 employees) and general plant superintendent, who usually has charge of plant personnel in an entire state.

Mr. Nagel is a case in point. He graduated from Beaumont High School in St. Louis in 1933, joining Southwestern Bell Telephone Company in 1936 after a period as a member of the St. Louis Cardinals' famed "knothole gang" and as a clerk for a hardware jobber. His boss warned him against going with the telephone company, saying he would "get lost in the shuffle" in the big company.

Mr. Nagel began digging ditches to bury a conduit. Each ditch was a spade wide and forty inches deep—a job now fortunately done almost entirely by machines. In the next few years he became a cable splicer's helper, lineman, cable splicer and installer. During this time he went to night school, taking a course in electronics.

In 1944 he went into the military service, where his experience led the Army to put him in charge of telephone service at Fort Sam Houston in Texas. Released from the service in 1946, he returned to Southwestern Bell as a facilities engineer designing outside plant installations. It was his first manager's job.

Promotions came rapidly. In the next three years he was named installation foreman, repair foreman in the downtown St. Louis area and then supervising installations foreman. During this period he tried to broaden his abilities by taking liberal arts courses at Washington University and St. Louis University.

In 1950 the company enrolled him in a human relations training course to improve his ability to deal with subordinates, then named him plant superintendent in a small district in Moberly, Missouri. From there, Mr. Nagel, along with 16 other district and division level managers, was sent to the University of Pennsylvania for a one-year course in liberal and fine arts. Upon its completion in 1954, he was made plant superintendent in Kansas City, Missouri. Two years later he was division plant superintendent for Eastern Missouri.

Still his training continued. In 1964 he was brought to the AT&T headquarters in New York for experience that would give him a broader view of the business. His initial appointment was as supervisor of repair service nationwide. Then, in 1966, he took over plant organization supervision, by which he helps member Bell companies with recruiting and other personnel problems.

While pleased with his own progress, Mr. Nagel likes to cite three men, all high school graduates, who attended installer's school with him. One is operations vice-president for the Chesapeake and Potomac Bell Telephone Companies. Another is territorial vice-president over Long Island and Queens, New York. The third is vice-president and general manager of Southwestern Bell.

The logical question to ask Mr. Nagel is why his old boss in the hardware business was wrong? Why didn't he get lost in the shuffle? "Any man who has enthusiasm and desire to progress stands head and shoulders above the crowd," he said. "If you want to do a good job and do the best you can, people can't help but notice you."

With the fantastic growth of the telephone business in the last quarter century, Bell System companies have refined techniques to discover and train managers. The latest personnel practices are used, including computers, to record and systematize all available information about employees. Management development courses are offered regularly to train potential managers. Foremen and other supervisors are urged constantly to search for men with leadership potential.

The search for talent, both for skilled craftsmen and managers, is the hallmark of most business and industrial firms today. There is a pronounced shortage of both, but the telephone industry perhaps tries harder because its executives believe that theirs is a business that cannot be learned as theory. It must be learned by doing it. A high school graduate can ask for no better opportunity.

The path from unskilled laborer to technician which has been described in this and the preceding chapter can be duplicated in nearly every industry which has a technological base. Let's look at just one more.

The industrial chemical industry is one of the largest, fastest growing and most innovative. Over half a million men and women are employed in the manufacture of more than 10,000 products. The industry produces organic and inorganic chemicals which are sold as raw materials to other manufacturers to use in their products. Chemical companies also make paint, fertilizers, drugs and other products which are sold directly to consumers.

A chemical plant in no way resembles an electronics plant, yet in a sense they are similar in their complexity. A chemical plant deals in molecules, combining and rearranging those found in products like coal, air and water to produce entirely different products, such as fabrics, dyes, perfume and thousands of others. Chemical plants are a forest of towers, tanks and buildings joined by a maze of pipes. The processes that are carried out in the plants are intricate and technical, and they must be carefully designed and rigidly controlled. Testing and analysis is a way of life.

So special are the processes and the equipment that each chemical company tends to train its own skilled workmen. They start with unskilled high school graduates and train them over a period of years to be equipment operators, men who measure the exact amount of materials to be processed and control such factors as temperature and pressure. To become a skilled operator, a person may go through a long apprentice period in which he gains experience as a laborer, helper and assistant operator.

The nature of a chemical plant, such as its use of acids and other corrosive materials, means that a great deal of maintenance must be performed. Again chemical companies prefer to train their own maintenance men, starting with unskilled high school graduates and training them to be pipefitters, machinists, electricians, instrument repairmen and other specialists. Sometimes one man may perform one or more of these specialties.

The technological nature of the chemical industry means

that a great many chemists and chemical engineers are hired, all of whom need technicians to assist them in research and development and in production control. Laboratory analysis must be performed constantly, usually by lab technicians. Some technicians come from colleges and technical schools, but most are high school graduates who have been trained by the companies, both on the job and in classrooms.

For the person with the interest and aptitude, "technician" may well be the magic word. It has the ring of the future to it. We have seen how the unskilled can become technicians, but there are other ways. The military service provides a steppingstone to technology for thousands annually. Military training in sonar, radar, radio repair and operations, telephone service, electronics, chemical warfare and many other fields have enabled men to be accepted as technicians after their service period is ended.

There are many good schools which also train technicians. An ambitious high school graduate can usually attend such schools part time while continuing to work. Attending extra classes is a good idea. Just because you aren't going to college is no reason why you have to end your education.

Chapter 4

Wanted: Servicemen Technicians

In the Spring of 1965, Clarence McNeil, educational program consultant for IBM, projected that the business machine and computer industry would need to add 65,000 technicians to its payroll through 1969. These were additional technicians. Replacements for those who resign or retire were not counted in this estimate. This computation had particular significance because at that time only 45,000 technicians of all types were being graduated annually from two-year technical colleges. This meant that the business machine and computer industry would need almost a third of the graduates, impossible considering the competition for technicians, the industry would have to train a great many of its own.

Early in 1967, less than two years later, Mr. McNeil refigured his estimates, discovering that the industry was likely to need 241,000 technicians between 1967 and 1976 —double his former estimate.

The industry realizes it has a very serious problem. It must train tens of thousands of technicians annually. This, of course, creates opportunities for high school graduates.

We have shown how high school graduates can go from unskilled production workers to technicians in the manufacturing part of the industry. There is a correspondingly greater need for technicians to maintain and repair business

machines which have been sold or rented to customers—
electric typewriters, dictation equipment, calculating machines, billing machines, duplicating equipment, addressing
machines and several types of cash registers. There are
thousands of different varieties of business machines marketed in the United States and more being developed all the
time. Virtually all of this equipment is electromechanical—
that is, the machines are electrically powered and thus have
motors, wiring and similar apparatus, yet they contain complex mechanical equipment. Many have electronic components.

The problem of the industry, as explained by Mr. McNeil,
is that until very recently no public or private educational
institutions trained electromechanical technicians. They
trained electronic technicians or mechanical technicians,
but no one who was expert in both specialities. Recently,
the industry has had success in urging technical schools
to establish "cross discipline" curricula to train the new type
of technician.

An example of the curricula comes from the University of
Oklahoma, which has established an experimental electromechanical technology course under a Federal grant. Five
types of courses are prepared in this guide: electrical-
electronic courses; mechanical courses; electromechanical
courses; physics and auxiliary courses; mathematics and
general education courses. Thus, in his first term a student
might study atomic and molecular structure, use of hand
tools, introduction to electromechanical systems, basic
energy systems, trigonometry. In his third term he might
study logic, circuits and systems, gears and gear trains,
servomotors and generators, transmissions and Boolean
algebra.

Eventually such cross discipline courses will be established and taught uniformly, but it will be many years, if

ever, before public and private colleges train sufficient electromechanical technicians. Meanwhile, the industry continues to train many thousands of high school graduates to be such technicians.

IBM, for example, expends at least as much effort in recruiting qualified high school graduates to become "customer engineers," as the servicemen are called, as it does recruiting scientific and engineering personnel. There can be no doubt that IBM is looking for a rather unusual individual. John J. Morrison, assistant in the Customer Engineering Department of IBM's Office Products Division, explains that the customer engineer is a "second salesman." When IBM sells its electric typewriters or other office products to a customer, it frequently also sells a service agreement which pledges the company to regularly inspect, maintain and repair the company products.

The customer engineer who performs these functions has a territory, a group of customers on whom he calls regularly, inspecting and repairing equipment. But he is unlike most servicemen. He wears a business suit, and his "tool bag" is an attaché case. He visits business offices and works beside executives, secretaries and stenographers. Thus, IBM is looking for a young man with maturity, dignity and personality.

He also must have a knack for working with his hands, and the desire and ability to make things work. The applicant is expected to have a thorough knowledge of electrical-mechanical principles and understanding of electrical-mechanical terminology sufficient to read and understand technical service manuals. He should also have enough knowledge of basic math to read and understand various simple gauges and measurement devices. IBM confronts the same difficulty that was described by Mr. Boardman of the Western Electric Company. Most high school graduates do not receive the proper educational background unless they take academic courses or attend vocational courses. IBM, like Western Electric, is encouraging changes in high school curricula, so that the general student who does not go on to college can receive the educational background that will be useful to him in the technological industries. Mr. McNeil suggests that the curricula include applied mathematics, physics, mechanics and mechanical drawing, electricity and electronics, logic and problem solving and interpersonal relationships to develop maturity. He maintains that such courses would not mean high schools are training electromechanical technicians. Rather, they would be providing the student with the background so the industry could turn him into a technician more easily.

The demand for high school graduates to become customer engineers in the business machine and computer industry already exceeds the supply and is growing rapidly. For example, the nation is just on the threshold of the teleprocessing era. Teleprocessing equipment will permit a large corporation to provide centralized computer services for all its branches. Equipment will be installed in a branch office, factory or store which will permit operators there to have instant contact by voice or teletypewriter over telephone lines with a central computer. Information could be fed into the computer and replies received in a matter of seconds. The equipment is not restricted to large corporations. Small businesses which normally would not invest in expensive computers will be able to take advantage of computer services by installing teleprocessing equipment. There are several types of such equipment—the Bell System calls theirs the Data-Phone Service. A minor revolution in business practices is expected. Banks and offices which now operate their own calculating equipment will be able to have instant central record keeping by use of teleprocessing equipment. A major effect on employment of business machine operators is anticipated in the years ahead.

Teleprocessing equipment will create a need for electromechanical servicemen. Even as this is being written, IBM is setting up experimental programs to accelerate the training of high school graduates to service teleprocessing equipment. It is too early to speculate how successful these programs will be, but it is certain that many thousands of teleprocessing equipment servicemen will be trained in the years ahead.

How do you become a customer engineer or a serviceman of electromechanical equipment? As described by Mr. Morrison the process is basically the same as for any job. An application is filled out. There is a careful interview. Aptitude tests are administered. But, as has been indicated, the individual sought by IBM must have good appearance, maturity and personality in addition to aptitude. "We want young men with an outward personality, who have the ability to deal with people," Mr. Morrison says.

Apply at any IBM branch office. The trainee is normally assigned there, although transfers are possible. After he is hired, he begins a self-pace training program at a local IBM office. This is not conventional classroom training. The student receives training material covering all basic IBM office products. This material is supported by audio-visual aids and actual IBM equipment. The rate of advancement depends on the individual. An instructor—an experienced customer engineer—is available if help is needed, but basically the student learns on his own, spending more time with those problems he finds most difficult. After completing the course, usually in three to four months, he is sent to a company plant at Lexington, Kentucky, for a final testing and orientation period, usually lasting two weeks. Then he is assigned to a branch office to begin calling on customers as an associate customer engineer. He receives close supervision until he qualifies for promotion to customer engineer in about two years.

The customer engineer is responsible for service in his territory, which can range from a large geographic area over which he drives to ones as small as a couple of floors in a midtown office building. Wherever his territory, he calls upon customers regularly to inspect and service machines. He is on call for emergencies and sometimes carries a radio beeper so that he can be reached at any time. He usually works a five-day, forty-hour week.

IBM has a career path for the customer engineer. He can advance to senior customer engineer, then take either of two paths, depending on his inclinations. In one path he becomes a technical specialist in some of the more complex products. In the other path, he may move into management as a territorial supervisor, field manager, branch manager for customer engineering or district manager for customer engineering. There are even high positions at the corporate level. Occasionally customer engineers will transfer into sales of office products or he can become a manufacturing technician.

Mr. Morrison is a product of this training himself. He became a customer engineer in White Plains, New York, in 1961 at age twenty-one with only a high school education. After advancing to Senior Customer Engineer, he was promoted to instructor at the Rochester, Minnesota, plant in 1966. A year later he was named field associate engineer at

Lexington, Kentucky. In 1969 he was promoted to field manager at Houston. In 1971, he was named senior staff assistant in the customer engineers department in the headquarters of the Office Products Division.

Even more startling is the career of Mr. McNeil, the corporate educational consultant. The day before he was interviewed, he had been in Washington, D. C., conferring with officials of the United States Office of Education about ways to improve the education of technicians. He consistently meets with top-ranking educators, university officials and industry leaders. Yet Mr. McNeil's only degree is a high school diploma. He is a native of Akron, Ohio, who graduated from Kenmore High School in 1940. After a period as a stock clerk in a Woolworth store and as a driver of a dry-cleaning delivery truck, he joined IBM in 1941 as a customer engineer trainee. His experience operating an auto repair garage with his brother had given him background for the job.

He finished his training in 1942 and was sent to Pittsburgh. He returned to Akron the following year. He spent three years in the military service, repairing office equipment in Europe. In 1946 Mr. McNeil was assigned a resident territory in Newcomerstown, Ohio, where he serviced IBM equipment for six years. He admits to feeling somewhat "forgotten," since he no longer worked out of a branch office. After a long chat with his superior about his career with the company, he was sent to Endicott, New York, as an instructor in the Customer Engineering School there.

From then on it was onward and upward for him, but in education rather than in service. Starting in 1955, he was plant coordinator of manufacturing training, then program manager of training at Endicott. In 1962 he moved to the corporate headquarters in Armonk, New York, as program administrator for educational operations, then two years later into his present post.

Mr. McNeil still has no college degree, although he attended classes at Akron University and Harper College in Endicott. But in his work he has organized and conducted many educational programs and read so much that he feels he has done at least enough work to qualify for a master's degree. He is living proof that even in the technological industry, which places so much emphasis on scientific and engineering skills, it is not the length of a man's education that counts. Rather it is what he can do with the education he has. In fact, at IBM there is a vast lore of stories about production workers, students and technicians who have made important contributions to technology.

Other companies train service engineers in different fashions. Some companies are set up to perform more of the repair work in shops. They are able to train young men in the shops for a year or so before sending them out to call on customers in offices and institutions.

A high school graduate who has the interest and aptitude certainly ought to consider a career servicing business machines and computers. It is a unique opportunity to learn a marketable skill in an industry that is attuned to the future. In addition to servicing electric typewriters and teleprocessing equipment, an individual may specialize in nonelectric typewriters, adding machines, calculating machines (which have complex mechanisms that add, subtract, divide, multiply and perform combinations of these operations), cash registers, accounting-bookkeeping machines (which post entries, do billing and perform many other functions), data-processing equipment (such as computers, tabulators, card punchers, sorters, collators, converters, tape transports and printers), dictating machines, duplicating and copying machines and postage and mailing equipment.

Chapter 5

Training for Mechanics
and Repairmen

Our mechanized age provides many opportunities for the high school graduate to learn a marketable skill as a repairman of the appliances and machines by which modern Americans order their lives. There are already three million people (mostly men) employed in more than 200 service occupations, yet this is one of the fastest-growing occupational areas in the country.

A career as a mechanic or repairman offers several advantages. There is usually a shortage of skilled men, so there is plenty of opportunity for employment. The repair industry is not as affected by economic slumps as many manufacturing industries, again enhancing employment. There tends to be less shift work, and in many of the repair specialties the working conditions are clean and comfortable. Earnings are on a par with those in manufacturing. Perhaps the most appealing aspect of a career in repairing is that it affords an excellent opportunity to go into business for oneself. Many a mechanic or serviceman has opened his own shop.

Most major manufacturers of appliances, vehicles and other products offer training programs. Formal apprenticeships are available, as are courses in technical and correspondence schools. But millions of young men have learned these skills informally by working in a garage or repair shop and even as a hobby.

So far, we have examined two types of repairmen in discussing the technological industry, the telephone repairman and the business machine and computer serviceman. The giant of the repair occupations is automobile mechanic. Over 600,000 are employed in the various auto repair specialties, with another 100,000 employed as auto body repairmen and 85,000 as diesel mechanics. About twenty-five per cent of the mechanics are employed in service departments of new and used car dealers. About forty per cent work in independent garages and shops. The remainder work in gasoline service stations; for organizations such as truck and bus companies, which operate fleets of vehicles and for Federal, state and local governments. Most auto repair shops employ from one to five mechanics, but some have more than a hundred. Opportunities for training and employment are available in almost every community in the nation.

There are several types of mechanics. Because of the increasing complexity of modern cars, mechanics tend to specialize in repairing motors, transmissions, brake systems, ignitions, auto bodies, exhaust systems, radiators, suspension systems and several others. A mechanic may further specialize in repair of just one or two makes of car. There are still general mechanics who repair any of a car's mechanical troubles, but the trend is clearly away from this. In fact an increasing number of today's garages use technology in repairing cars. Automobile "clinics" are being erected around the country which apply as many as eighty-six tests to a vehicle. Electronic equipment automatically tests the ignition system and measures braking power, wheel balance and alignment and the carburetor functions. The precise diagnosis which results permits mechanics to make the correct repairs. Much of the diagnostic guesswork is being removed from the garage business.

A young person should expect to train to be an auto mechanic. Many men have become automobile mechanics with insufficient training. There is little room for guesswork. To be a good mechanic, a man can only learn by doing, yet there is need to know theory and the standards built into the car by the manufacturer.

One does not become a mechanic casually. Tinkering with a jalopy in the family driveway does not qualify one to work on the engine of an expensive eight cylinder car. Just because one can do a "valve job" on one make of car does not mean he is qualified to do the same task on another make, nor does it make him an expert on ignition systems in any car. To become a good automobile mechanic, a young man should be prepared to study manuals, take courses and learn on the job through carefully programmed instruction. One of the best ways to do this is through the four-year apprenticeship program available in many communities. The Armed Forces also train automobile mechanics, but additional training is usually needed to accommodate their skills to civilian vehicles. Indeed, a skilled mechanic ought to be prepared never to stop learning, for as the new models come out each year there is always something new to learn.

The time-honored way to become a skilled mechanic is to start as a helper, lubrication man, car washer, gas station attendant or some similar job in a garage, then learn the trade by working with experienced mechanics. The length of time required to learn the skills depends upon a person's aptitude, but three to four years would certainly be an average.

Mechanics' wages vary widely, from as low as the minimum wage, in some communities, to as high as $10,000 a year for top men. There are advancement opportunities. In a large shop a mechanic may become a foreman, service salesman or service manager. Mechanics move into the parts department or even into new and used car sales. And, of course, many mechanics open their own garage or gas station.

The second largest group of repairmen are the maintenance electricians, numbering more than 250,000. These are experts who install, modify, maintain and repair such electrical equipment as motors, transformers, generators, circuit breakers, controls and lighting equipment in industrial, commercial and public facilities. He is a skilled individual who works with wiring, fuses, transformers, coils and switches. He splices wires and installs conduits. He must be familiar with such devices as ammeters, volt-ohmmeters and oscilloscopes. He must be able to read blueprints accurately and make mathematical computations relating to load capacities and connections for electrical wiring.

About 55 per cent of the maintenance electricians are employed to service equipment and machinery used in manufacturing plants. Other large employers include transportation, communications and public utility firms, stores, mines and government. Some are employed by electrical repair firms which provide service for a number of small businesses and industries. The skilled maintenance electrician is usually in great demand, and his abilities are transferable to many different industries with a minimum of retraining. But, again, no one ever learns enough in this fast-changing industry. Many electricians have learned electronics to keep pace with the changing technology.

The best way to become a maintenance electrician is through a four-year apprentice program. This blends theory, blueprint reading and necessary mathematics with programmed on-the-job training. But many men have become skilled by starting as helpers and working beside skilled workers. Many large industries offer formal courses for young men. In the latter case, a high school background which includes algebra, trigonometry, physics, electricity and basic science is recommended.

Thousands of openings are expected in each of the next ten years. Maintenance electricians will be particularly sought after in the metal, machinery and chemical industries.

The third largest group of repairmen are those who service appliances, such as refrigerators, stoves, laundry equipment, toasters, vacuum cleaners and scores of other "gadgets" familiar to all of you. About 220,000 are employed in this occupation, but it is growing so rapidly such a figure can only an estimation.

The appliance repairman works in every city and town. Most men are employed by independent repair shops, but appliance dealers, department stores and other firms that sell appliances provide many jobs. Gas and electric utility companies are another large employer. Wherever he is employed, the appliance serviceman usually visits the customer in his home or place of business, making repairs there or giving estimates and taking the appliance back to the shop. They frequently drive light trucks or automobiles to make their rounds.

Appliances are not nearly so complex as business machines, telephone equipment and other electromechanical equipment, but considerable expertise is required nonetheless. Small appliances such as toasters and food mixers are usually the simplest to repair, with large appliances such as refrigerators and washing machines being the most difficult. Repairs usually involve replacing parts, cleaning, fixing electrical connections and adjusting the motor.

There is no formal apprenticeship program, so appliance servicing must be learned on the job. The inexperienced man is usually given simpler assignments, such as helping to install appliances and driving vehicles. Then he may begin repairing appliances in the shop, starting with simple tasks (replacing a switch) and progressing to more difficult ones. Training lasts six months to a year before a man is permitted to make house calls. It usually takes three years to become a fully qualified serviceman. Night school and correspondence courses in basic electricity can only help the process.

In addition to aptitude, appliance repair shops look for men who have an attractive appearance and an outgoing personality, necessary when dealing with customers in their homes. Character references are almost always checked carefully. In large shops, a man may be promoted to foreman, or service manager. There is always the opportunity to go into business for oneself.

Few occupations provide the opportunities for employment that appliance repair does. Owning appliances is almost a national preoccupation, creating a great demand for service. There will be many thousands of job openings annually in the foreseeable future.

A related occupation is television and radio repairing, in which about 130,000 men are employed. In addition to TV and radio, these men service phonographs, hi-fi equipment, tape recorders, public address systems and two-way mobile radios.

Working in this occupation requires a high level of expertise. Vocational or trade school training, home correspondence courses or an active hobby as a "ham" radio operator are virtually essential. Even when a person has the necessary theoretical background, two to three years of additional on-the-job and technical training is necessary to become skilled. Manufacturers of radio and television equipment provide a great deal of training in special classes and in manuals published for their various products.

In their work, repairmen use a variety of tools and test equipment to diagnose the breakdown in the set. They normally eliminate each possible cause of the trouble, using vacuum tube voltmeters, oscilloscopes, signal generators and other equipment to zero in on the difficulty.

Employment opportunities will remain good in this field, but the trend is toward more expert repairmen as manufacturers make sets which, while developing fewer service problems, are more complex.

Another specialty experiencing rapid growth is repairing air-conditioning and refrigeration equipment. About 115,-000 are now so employed. Use of air conditioning in offices, factories, institutional buildings and private residences is growing rapidly all over the country, and the need for repairmen is keeping pace. Installation is an important part of this work, from the small room air conditioner to the huge unit serving an entire building. After installation, equipment needs regular maintenance and repair. The repairman must be skilled in mechanics, electrical motors, piping, filters, pumps, dehumidifiers and other components.

Many air-conditioning mechanics work for shops that specialize in such equipment. Other employers are construction companies, equipment manufacturers and dealers. Some are employed by stores, hotels, restaurant chains, warehouses and other large users of air conditioning.

Most mechanics start as helpers and acquire skills by working with experienced men. They gradually take over more complicated tasks and eventually begin to make service calls.

There are a variety of mechanics who work on industrial

and mobile machinery. Diesel mechanics specialize in maintenance, repair or rebuilding of diesel engines of bulldozers, tractors and other equipment used on highways and farms and in industry. Employers are usually distributors and dealers of such equipment or bus, trucking or construction firms and others which operate fleets of diesel-powered equipment.

There are several ways to learn the trade. One is through formal apprentice programs usually lasting four years. Apprenticeships are usually available through diesel engine manufacturers. Other mechanics first learn to repair gasoline-powered engines and then transfer to diesel equipment. Still others learn on the job, starting as helpers.

Use of diesel equipment is increasing. Employment opportunities in this mechanical specialty appear to be excellent.

About 180,000 men are employed by industry to install, maintain and repair heavy industrial equipment. The type of machinery on which they work varies with the industry, but the big employers are in the food, primary metals, machinery manufacturing, chemical, fabricated metal products and transportation equipment industries.

There are formal apprenticeship programs, but many men learn the skills informally in the maintenance department of industries. They begin as helpers or oilers and progress under the guidance of experienced men. This is another speciality with good growth prospects, as the use of machinery in industry is increasing.

An honored craft is that of the millwright, who moves and installs heavy industrial machinery, using hoists, cranes and other rigging devices. In assembling machinery they fit bearings, gears and belts and attach motors. They frequently work in a maintenance team which includes pipefitters and machinery repairmen.

About half the 80,000 millwrights are employed in the steel, paper, machinery and automobile manufacturing industries. Other major employers are construction, lumber, chemicals and fabricated metal products.

There are apprentice programs lasting four years, but many millwrights learn informally, starting as helpers. Courses in mathematics, mechanical drawing and machine shop practices are helpful.

Although it is not a large craft, a moderate increase in the number of millwrights is anticipated in the next decade.

From large heavy equipment, we go to the small, delicate devices. There will be excellent opportunities for instrument repairmen in the years ahead. Increasing automation and mechanization of industry has caused greater use of precise instruments to control heat, pressure, flow of liquids, chemical composition and other production factors. There are thousands of different instruments. They keep airplanes on course, measure electricity, control laboratory experiments and perform thousands of functions. Some of the instruments are highly complex, and all must operate to precise tolerances. Many mechanics specialize in certain types of instruments.

As might be anticipated, this is not a craft learned overnight. Technical schools offer curricula for such mechanics. There is a formal four-year apprenticeship program established. The Armed Forces train repairmen. Certain industries offer formal and on-the-job training courses for repairmen.

Chapter 6

Training for the Traditional Crafts

For generations, indeed hundreds of years, young men who have not gone into college have "learned a trade"—that is, they have entered formal training to become craftsmen in the building trades, machining occupations and certain other specialities, such as welding and boilermaking.

This is still true today. Many of the traditional trades, in particular the machining group, provide opportunities for many thousands of young men to learn a marketable skill. But in frankness it must be said that the traditional crafts are not the premium opportunities they once were. The technological industries, as we have seen, are training people to perform a variety of new skills. The burgeoning service industries are employing and training far greater numbers of high school graduates than the traditional crafts. Still, there is opportunity in these fields, and many young men are interested in them.

Members of the machining occupations appear likely to remain in great demand for many years to come, for almost every product of American industry is either made of metal or manufactured by machinery made of metal parts. The electronics industry, for example, may use relatively little metal in its transistors, but it depends heavily on machinists and tool and die makers to produce the tools and parts it needs for its processes and equipment.

About one and a quarter million men (only a few women) are employed in the machining occupations nationwide. About 530,000 are machinists, 425,000 are machine tool operators, 165,000 are tool and die makers and 70,000 are set-up men. Most are employed in the metalworking industries, and many thousands are trained annually. Nearly every industry which makes use of metal trains high school graduates in the machining trades.

A machining worker makes tools, dies and metal parts by operating a variety of metal-cutting equipment, including lathes and machines that grind, drill, mill, polish and buff, bore, shape and plane. The machine tools may be described as power-driven equipment which firmly holds the piece of metal that is to be shaped while the operator uses a cutting instrument (called a "tool") to cut, shave or otherwise shape the metal. The machining occupations are so highly skilled because many tools and parts have to be made to incredibly precise specifications. Sometimes metal parts are machined to within ten millionths of an inch. In addition, the operators have to set up their machinery, read blueprints and make computations in trigonometry.

The most highly skilled of the machining occupations is the tool and die maker. He performs the most precise work to the most exacting tolerances. The instrument makers who machine metal parts to great accuracy are also highly skilled. They often assemble and test instruments. The all-around machinist can operate a variety of equipment, but he is usually less skilled in fine tolerances than the tool and die maker. The greatest number of workers in the field are machine tool operators, who usually specialize in one type of tooling machine, making metal products of less

precise tolerances. Depending upon the product manufactured, machine tool operators can rank as skilled or
semiskilled workmen.

To become a machinist or a tool and die maker requires
a great deal of training and experience. Most industries
making use of metal train their own machining craftsmen. Training practices vary from industry to industry and
company to company according to needs, but for illustrative
purposes let's examine the training program at the Western
Electric Company plant in Kearny, New Jersey. It was
described by Kenneth J. Kubicki, a tool and die maker who
trained at the plant and is now coordinating supervisor
of technical education at the Kearny Works.

The toolmaker training school is the premier craft school
at Kearny. The manufacturing operations at the plant require a great many of the very finest tools and dies. Trainees
(Western Electric dislikes the word "apprentice" because
it seems to connote an indentured servant) are recruited
directly from high schools and from production workers. It
is quite difficult to qualify for the training course. A high
school graduate must pass a battery of five difficult tests
measuring his intelligence and comprehension and his
knowledge of mathematics, mechanics and physics.

Then the applicant is interviewed by the instructor of
the toolmaking course. He is a master craftsman, thoroughly
familiar with the demands of the occupation. At the very
least, being a tool and die maker requires discipline, maturity and high motivation. The toolmaker must have great
pride in his work and a compelling sense of perfection. The
interviewer looks for these qualities in the applicant.

To be accepted as a trainee, the applicant must also have
considerable expertise. He must know the "jargon," as Mr.
Kubicki puts it; that is, he must be familiar with the names
of the various cutting tools and other devices used by tool-

makers, and he must know the uses of the implements. He must have had mathematics through trigonometry, be able to read blueprints and be knowledgeable in use of the micrometer, an instrument which measures very small distances, angles and diameters.

A young man can achieve this level of skill through previous work experience (preferably at the Kearny plant) or in a machinist course in a vocational high school. Mr. Kubicki indicates that only the exceptional youngster can qualify for this premier course. He reported that of twenty-seven recent graduates of a vocational high school machine shop course only seven passed the tests and only two of those were accepted after interviews.

Despite the high entrance qualifications, the Kearny Works has twenty-six toolmakers in training at all times. To complete the course, the trainee must receive 140 credits, with one credit equaling approximately forty hours of successful work. The average trainee graduates in three and a half years. During his training the toolmaker learns to machine to ever finer tolerances. Mr. Kubicki said a typical trainee will be able to work at .005-inch tolerance upon completing high school. In six months he is expected to be working at .003-inch tolerances, then to .001 in a year, .0005 in a year and a half, and .0001 in two years. He is paid during his training. Upon completing the course, he becomes a toolmaker at the lowest level. A typical tool-maker may take five years to progress to the highest level.

Mr. Kubicki is certainly an individual who speaks well for the advantages of the toolmaking course. He doesn't remember when he decided to become a tool and die maker. "I was perhaps five years old—even younger," he recalls. "The most successful relative in my father's family was a tool and die maker, and I just grew up certain I would emulate him."

Mr. Kubicki graduated from Dickinson High School in New Jersey, having completed a three-and-a-half-year machinist's course, and was accepted as a toolmaking trainee at the Kearny Works. But he didn't do well at first. After six weeks the instructor told him he didn't know a thing about toolmaking and ought to consider another line of work. Instead of following the instructor's advice, however, Mr. Kubicki enrolled in the Stevens Institute of Technology in Hoboken, attending classes after working hours. He completed the three-year course in tool design in 1956. "This gave me a really good understanding of the theory of toolmaking," he says. That same year, he completed his apprentice program and became a toolmaker at Kearny.

In 1957 Mr. Kubicki matriculated at Seton Hall University, studying business management. Again he went to school after working hours. In 1960 he was promoted to supervising instructor of the toolmaking course—replacing the man who said he would never pass the course. Meanwhile, he transferred from Seton Hall to the Newark College of Engineering, studying tool design. In 1964 he was certified as a teacher of vocational education. At the same time, he returned to Seton Hall, eventually receiving his bachelor of science degree—continuing to work all the time.

But even before he received his college degree, Western Electric recognized Mr. Kubicki as a young man with a future. He was an expert tool and die craftsman who was capable of instructing others. Added to this he had procured knowledge about business management, personnel practices, finances and other subjects. Thus, to the surprise of no one, he was tapped in 1966 to join Mr. Boardman in the Community Relations division, helping schools develop their curricula so students would be better qualified to work in business and industry. Mr. Boardman says of his young assistant, "I consider it inevitable that he will some day be working on educational matters at the corporate level of American Telephone and Telegraph."

Mr. Kubicki is among the most impressive young executives I have ever met, an energetic, ambitious person who has added, by pure hard work, theoretical knowledge to his ability to work with his hands. It is a rare combination, but of great value to employers.

The toolmaking course at Kearny is very demanding, but the young person who completes it has learned a skill useful to him throughout his life.

There are other opportunities to learn a craft at Kearny. There is a machinist training school, which operates in the same manner as the toolmaking school, but the entrance requirements and the anticipated performance are more relaxed. Many young men who fail to qualify as toolmakers enter the machinist course. A draftsman school is also operated. Entrance requirements are two or more years of drafting in high school. Training takes place largely on the job, following a three week orientation course to familiarize the trainee with the methods used at Kearny. Another way a craft may be learned at the plant is as a plant trades helper, assisting qualified electricians, steamfitters, riggers and other tradesmen. Uusally one helper is assigned to three craftsmen. The training lasts until the helper has demonstrated the ability to perform as a craftsman and there is an opening in the maintenance force.

Every industry trains the craftsmen it needs in its operations. A major steel company, for example, offers apprenticeships in the following trades: electrician (wireman), electronic repairman, instrument repairman, lead burner, machinist, patternmaker, toolmaker, blacksmith, boilermaker, bricklayer, electrician (armature winder), electrician (shop), molder, roll turner, sheet metal worker, carpenter, coremaker, electrician (lineman), pipefitter, rigger, welder, painter, motor inspector, millwright. Most of these apprenticeships include from 6,240 to 8,320 hours of instruction with about one-tenth in the classroom and the remainder in shop work.

The rules governing apprenticeships in industrial plants are usually worked out between the company and the union. These rules spell out the qualifications of apprentices, testing procedures, curricula, wages and performance levels. Apprenticeship programs offer excellent opportunities to learn a skill, yet in some industries there is a problem. Apprentices, as members of the labor union, fall under the union seniority system. In those industries where employment fluctuates with production, apprentices tend to be the first workers laid off and the last to be recalled. This interrupts the continuity of their training. Both union and management officials indicate they are aware of this problem. Efforts are made to continue the apprenticeship training during periods of slack employment.

There are many crafts used in industry. There are a battery of skills involved in foundry and forging operations. Careers as welders and as oxygen and arc cutters will offer many thousands of job openings annually for the next decade. No young man should be discouraged from entering industrial crafts, but it should be pointed out that the opportunities are not as great as in some of the newer technological industries and in the service industries.

The same general statement applies to the traditional building trades. Most of you will be familiar with these, but let's review the major ones:

CARPENTERS—This is the largest of the building trades. Carpenters perform a wide variety of tasks. They erect the wood framework of buildings, and when the building is ready for trimming, they install molding, paneling, cabinets, window sashes, door frames, doors, floors, stairs and much more. They build docks, railroad trestles, frames to hold concrete until it hardens, erect scaffolding and do many other tasks in industry and in the construction of homes, buildings, bridges and highways. Carpenters tend to specialize in one form of woodworking, such as rough carpentry, floors or trimming.

PAINTERS AND PAPERHANGERS—These are separate crafts, but they are generally spoken of together. They prepare the interior and exterior surfaces of structures, then apply paint, varnish, enamel, lacquer, paper and other materials with brushes or spraying devices.

PLUMBERS AND PIPEFITTERS—These are similar crafts, but men tend to specialize in one or the other. In general, a pipefitter installs high- and low-pressure pipe that carries hot water, steam, liquids and gases, especially in industrial and commercial buildings. The plumber customarily connects residential and commercial facilities for water, gas or waste disposal to public utility systems.

BRICKLAYERS—These craftsmen construct walks, partitions, fireplaces, chimneys, buildings and many other structures made of brick. They work with conventional brick, concrete and glass block, tile, marble and terra cotta.

OPERATING ENGINEERS—These are the men who operate power-driven construction machinery, such as power shovels, cranes, derricks, hoists, pile drivers, concrete mixers, paving machines, trench and hole diggers, bulldozers, tractors and pumps. They tend to specialize in certain equipment.

ELECTRICIANS (CONSTRUCTION)—As you have observed, there are a variety of electricians employed in industry and construction. Electricians in the building trades lay out, assemble, install and test electrical wiring and fixtures used to provide heat, light, air conditioning and refrigeration in homes, apartment and commercial buildings, factories, hospitals, schools and other public buildings. They install switches, conduits, controls, wires, lights, signal equipment, circuit breakers and much more.

IRONWORKERS—There are several subspecialties, including structural, ornamental and reinforcing. The structural ironworkers erect the steel framework of buildings, bridges, tanks and overhead cranes. Ornamental ironworkers erect metal stairways, catwalks, floor gratings, metal sashes and doors, grills, screens, metal cabinets and safety deposit boxes, as well as decorative gates, fences and balconies. Reinforcing ironworkers, sometimes called rodmen, set steel bars in concrete forms to reinforce concrete structures.

PLASTERERS—These craftsmen apply plaster to interior walls and ceilings and stucco to the exterior of buildings.

ROOFERS—The task here is to apply the tile, slate or other suitable materials to the roofs of buildings. They also waterproof and dampproof structures.

CEMENT MASONS—These tradesmen finish exposed concrete surfaces. They may do small jobs such as concrete floors, patios and sidewalks, or work on huge dams, highways and foundations of skyscrapers.

FLOOR COVERING INSTALLERS—These are the men who install, repair and replace tiles, linoleum, carpeting and other materials used on the floors of homes, commercial and industrial buildings.

SHEET METAL WORKERS—The fabrication and installation of ducts used in ventilating, air-conditioning and heating systems is performed by these craftsmen. They also fabricate and install a variety of other equipment, such as shelves, partitions, kitchen equipment, storefronts and signs.

ASBESTOS AND INSULATING WORKERS—Their principal tasks are to cover pipes, boilers and other equipment with insulating material. Most work in commercial and industrial construction.

LATHERS—These men erect the supporting backs for walls and ceilings to which plaster or other materials are applied.

MARBLE SETTERS, TILE SETTERS AND TERRAZZO WORKERS—They cover interior and exterior walls, floor and other surfaces with the materials indicated by their skills. They tend to specialize in one of the materials. Laying the ceramic tile in bathrooms would be an example of their work.

GLAZIERS—Working with glass is the specialty of these craftsmen. They cut, fit and install plate glass, ordinary windows, mirrors and specialty items.

ELEVATOR CONSTRUCTION WORKERS—The name itself provides a description. These men assemble and install elevators, escalators, dumbwaiters and similar apparatus. They also maintain and repair them.

STONEMASONS—They build the stone exteriors of structures, primarily office buildings, hotels, churches and other public buildings. They work with natural stone, such as marble, granite and limestone, and with artificial stone made from cement or other materials.

The building tradesmen are associated with the construction industry. They are employed primarily by general contractors and subcontractors who specialize in one phase of construction. They are among the highest paid of all workmen—as much as six dollars an hour—but they do not work steadily. Employment fluctuates seasonally and with weather conditions. The number of jobs is directly controlled by the amount of construction activity, both nationwide and in specific localities. The volume of construction is frequently used as a barometer of economic conditions. Every construction worker has periods of unemployment after jobs are finished. Many lead a rather nomadic existence, moving from project to project around the country.

But construction is not the only source of employment for building tradesmen. The service industry employs several varieties, particularly plumbers, glaziers, sheet metal workers and electricians on a full-time basis. Industry hires many building craftsmen for its maintenance forces, particularly plumbers and pipefitters, electricians, ironworkers, roofers, bricklayers and carpenters. When craftsmen are employed full time, they are customarily paid at a lower wage than those men who work in construction.

Although less than other fields, the building trades will offer considerable opportunity for young men to learn a marketable skill in the next decade. The degree of opportunity varies from trade to trade. The demand for some skills is declining, while for others it is increasing. For example, the popularity of glass in modern construction is heightening the employment of glaziers, while stonemasons are less in demand because stone construction is not in vogue. The use of power equipment in construction, particularly with the highway building program, is creating a demand for operating engineers, while use of factory-built dry-wall is depressing employment of plasterers.

All of the building trades seem to be in a state of flux. The new technology has not yet made its effect on construction, but change seems to be inevitable. Anachronistic building codes are being rewritten to permit the use of new metals, plastics and other materials, as well as new pre-fabricated construction techniques which may greatly alter the employment patterns. The trend toward aluminum or steel "curtain wall" for exterior walls seems likely to continue, as does the use of prefabricated concrete elements.

The United States Bureau of Labor Statistics has sought to estimate the demand for the various building trades through the mid-1970s. The bureau has provided figures for the number of workers who will be needed to replace crafts-men who resign or retire, as well as estimate the over-all growth of the trade. The following table comprises these estimates and includes the length of the apprenticeship.

Examination of this table will permit some evaluation of the opportunities in the various trades. It should be remembered that the bureau predicated its estimates on continuation of high levels of construction activity. It should also be noted that these are nationwide estimates. The hiring of 1,000 replacement workers a year is not very many when spread over 50 states.

The recommended way to enter the building trades is through the apprenticeship program. Rules vary, but, in general, apprentices are required to be between the ages of eighteen and twenty-five and in good physical condition. They should have a high school education or its equivalent, with courses in mathematics and sciences desirable. Aptitude tests are administered routinely.

Apprenticeships usually last from two to five years. During this time the apprentice receives a minimum of 144 hours a year of formal classroom training in such subjects as history of the trade, characteristics of materials used, applicable mathematics, engineering principles, sketching and drafting, blueprint reading and safety practices. Most of

Craft	Number Employed	Annual Replacement Needs	Estimated Growth	Years of Apprenticeship
Carpenters	830,000	20,000	Rapid	4
Painters and Paperhangers	385,000	10,000	Rapid	3
Plumbers and Pipefitters	350,000	7-8,000	Rapid	5
Bricklayers	175,000	3,000	Rapid	3
Operating Engineers	310,000	5-6,000	Very Rapid	3
Electricians	190,000	3,000	Very Rapid	4 or 5
Ironworkers	85,000	Hundreds	Rapid	3
Plasterers	35,000	Hundreds	Slow	3 or 4
Roofers	60,000	Hundreds	Rapid	3
Cement Masons	65,000	1,000	Very Rapid	3
Floor Covering Installers	40,000	Hundreds	Moderate	3 or 4
Sheet Metal Workers	60,000	Hundreds	Rapid	4
Asbestos Insulating Workers	25,000	500	Moderate	4
Lathers	30,000	Hundreds	Rapid	2
Marble Setters, etc.	30,000	Hundreds	Moderate	3
Glaziers	10,500	Hundreds	Very Rapid	3
Elevator Construction	15,000	Hundreds	Moderate	2
Stonemasons	N. A.	Small	Slight	3

the training occurs on the job under the guidance of foremen, master craftsmen and experienced journeymen. The apprentice does work of increasing difficulty, and his earnings increase with his ability. Generally he receives half the journeyman's wage rate.

In most communities the apprenticeship programs are supervised by a joint committee consisting of employers and union officials. The committee establishes the rules, entrance requirements, curriculum and wages. It arranges for the continuity of training for the apprentice, who may be moved around to various employers in the locality to ensure that he learns all phases of the trade. Upon completion of his apprenticeship, the trainee is certified as a journeyman. In those trades where it is appropriate, such as electricians and plumbers, he is licensed to practice his trade.

Not all who become building craftsmen go through the formal apprenticeship program. Many learn informally by working for years as helpers, observing and being taught by experienced men. Some have learned their skills in part by attending vocational or trade schools or by taking correspondence courses.

As a rule, laborers, particularly those on large construction projects, do not receive an opportunity to learn a trade. There are about 700,000 members of the laborers and hod-carriers union who do manual labor such as loading and unloading materials, carrying and stacking equipment, grading and shoveling. But these men seldom get a chance to assist the craftsmen or to use their tools.

Chapter 7

Opportunities for Production Workers

A generation ago a young man or woman had an excellent opportunity to find employment as an unskilled or semi-skilled laborer in the production departments of manufacturing plants. He or she found a job on the production line of a factory, assembling or operating equipment that required little training and developed only limited skills. He might have become a good drill press operator or tire molder, but he could not perform maintenance functions or operate other equipment without retraining. He could market his abilities only in the same industry which operated the same equipment.

Are there opportunities for unskilled and semiskilled workers today?

If you read the newspapers and magazines, you are aware of the decline in the number of production jobs. Much is written about automation, a loosely used term which appears to refer to the fact that some industries are discovering it is cheaper to have machines do routine jobs than it is to hire workers. There is no doubt that manufacturing equipment, particularly in newer plants, is increasing the amount of production performed by the individual workers, and that many of the tasks formerly done by unskilled and semi-skilled workers are now performed by machines.

The extent of automation is perhaps overemphasized. There are still many production jobs for the unskilled, but every manpower study indicates that unskilled and semi-skilled job opportunities are declining. This trend is expected to accelerate.

The 1972 Manpower Report of the United States Department of Labor estimated the demands for various categories of workers between 1970 and 1980 and compared this growth to the 1960-70 period. The study showed that in the 1960s, the number of farmers and farm workers declined by about 40 per cent. In the next decade the decline should be almost 17 per cent.

The employment of nonfarm laborers—that is, those working as unskilled laborers in factories and service industries, increased about 5 per cent between 1960 and 1970—but is expected to *decline* by 6 per cent in the next 10 years. The only opportunities are for replacement of unskilled workers who resign, retire, die or move on to other jobs.

The number of semiskilled machinery operators increased about 16 per cent in the 1960s, but in the 1970s the increase is expected to be only about 10 per cent.

Contrast these estimates with those fields where great growth is expected. By 1980, about 15 million workers will be needed in the professional and technical occupations —40 per cent more than in 1970. By 1980, there are expected to be 17 million clerical workers, almost one-quarter more than in 1970. Another 13 million people are expected to be service workers, a third more than in 1970.

Among the manual workers, skilled craftsmen will have the most rapid increases in employment in the last half of the decade. Their number may rise from 10 million in

1970 to 12.2 million in 1980, with the greatest growth anticipated for mechanics and repairmen.

There is only one message in these statistics—develop a marketable skill.

But many of you are legitimately interested in working in industrial production. Laboring and semiskilled entry-level jobs are, as we have seen, often stepping stones to technical and skilled positions. Many find semiskilled production work highly satisfying. Working conditions are often pleasant. Many men and women do not desire the responsibility and "headaches" that accompany skilled work and supervisory positions. This is perhaps a good time to say that although the purpose of this book is to emphasize the opportunities for skill development, there is absolutely no intent to be condescending toward those individuals who find satisfaction in simpler tasks.

Those of you who take jobs as unskilled production workers in the hope of becoming supervisors and managers or of learning a marketable skill have some obstacles to overcome. A major one is the union seniority system. There is no intent here to criticize the system, merely to state the situation. Seniority has a worthwhile purpose and is to be commended. It ensures that a man who has been doing a particular job for the longest time receives the first opportunity to be promoted to a better position. It is only fair, and it is difficult to think of a more desirable way to maintain a flow of experienced workmen.

No system is perfect, however. The trouble with the seniority system is that it thwarts the younger, newer employee who is ambitious and has aptitude. He may have to wait so many years for his chance for training or promotions that he gives up. His ambition is stifled or he leaves the business for one offering more opportunity. Neither management nor union like to see this happen. The company is looking for men to train and promote, and the union realizes its strength and the well-being of its membership lies in having as many skilled workers as possible.

Union and management have tried to solve the problem by inserting the word "qualified" in the seniority rules. The verbiage varies, but in general the rules specify that the promotion will go to the qualified man with the most seniority. This does not thwart the chance of the senior man, yet it gives the talented youngster a chance to prove he is more qualified.

To be pragmatic about it, if the company elevates a junior man over a senior man, it must be able to prove to the union's satisfaction that the junior man is more qualified. If you are that junior man, it is up to you to provide the company with the proof of your superior qualifications.

How do you prove you are more qualified than a senior man? There are many ways. Your production record is superior. You have received a series of good reports from your supervisors. You have shown interest, leadership, motivation and cooperation. You have requested transfers to other jobs. Most importantly, you have prepared yourself. You have taken courses which give you a background peculiarly suitable for the better job. You took these courses in high school, perhaps, or you enrolled in voluntary education courses offered by the company. Perhaps you took some night courses in an appropriate technical school or you completed home-study courses. Your hobbies, your "moonlighting" jobs, your previous work experience, can all add to your qualifications.

The point is that providing the proof of your qualifications is up to you. The company testing procedures will indicate that you have special aptitudes, perhaps, but potential is not enough. Performance, education and experience are what count.

Henry Boardman, the Western Electric Company executive who was quoted earlier, had some sage advice for ambitious young men and women entering production fields. You should be as specific as possible about the job as you desire, he said. If you walk into the employment office and ask for any job, that is what you get—any job. But if you know the jobs for which you could qualify and show an interest in being trained, you may well receive the opportunity. Describe yourself as fully as you can, your interests, experience, hobbies, talents. You may never know when something you consider unimportant may create an opportunity. Mr. Boardman likes to tell about the production worker who turned a photographic hobby into a job as plant photographer. Another favorite story concerns the foreman who was put in charge of shipping goldfish from the company reflecting pool because he let it be known that he raised and shipped tropical fish for a hobby.

Yet you should be realistic. At the time of your employment for production jobs, you will probably receive rather short treatment. There are many people to be hired and not much time to spend with each one. Your chance to prove yourself comes later—and the people who hired you haven't much to do with your career development. Mr. Boardman also speaks of the "tyranny of time and place." There may be a wonderful job for you in Topeka, Kansas, but if you live in Birmingham, Alabama, the fact does not do you much good. There may be a job for which you are particularly qualified open at the plant where you are applying, but if the person just ahead of you fills it, you know what is meant by the tyranny of time.

But the most important part of your future rests with

selling yourself to your immediate supervisor. This is done by handling some of his problems for him, by being willing to volunteer and by solving your own problems. Yet it is important that you ask for help when you really need it. A costly mistake because you were too shy or stubborn or overconfident hardly makes a good impression. Mostly it is done by showing a high level of performance. Selling yourself to your supervisor requires some tact and judgment, too. If you try too hard and act like an "apple polisher," you will hurt your chances. Your supervisor won't like it, nor will your fellow workers.

Employment opportunities vary by industry and even with individual companies within an industry. In the remainder of this chapter, the employment outlook in representative industries, as estimated by the Bureau of Labor Statistics, will be reported.

The iron and steel industry employs about 629,000 people, four-fifths of whom are plant workers. Almost half of the plant workers are semiskilled and one-fifth unskilled. Skilled workers and foremen compose approximately three-tenths of a plant force. New workers are usually hired at the unskilled levels, progressing to the skilled jobs on a seniority basis. Thus, to become a blast furnace blower, you might start as a laborer, advancing to cinderman or slagger, keeper's helper, keeper, blower's helper and finally to blower. In the open-hearth department, you would begin doing general clean-up work around the furnace, then advance to third helper, second helper, first helper and eventually to blower. Over-all steel employment is expected to increase, but largely in the clerical, sales, engineering and research and development branches. There also will be increases in the maintenance force. A gradual decline in the less skilled production jobs is anticipated, despite increases in steel production, because of the adoption of automatic machinery and equipment which permits larger batches to be produced with the same manpower. Employment in the industry fluctuates widely with changes in business conditions. Production workers are affected most adversely during layoffs.

The motor vehicle manufacturing industry employs about 810,000 workers. About 90 per cent of the production of automobiles, trucks, buses and repair parts is centered in ten states. Michigan alone accounts for nearly 40 per cent of total employment. Ohio, Indiana, Wisconsin and New York have another third of the production. Other major producers of motor vehicles are California, Missouri, Illinois, New Jersey and Pennsylvania. Workers in assembling, inspecting, materials handling and other semiskilled plant jobs comprise nearly half the workers. Another quarter are employed as foremen, mechanics and repairmen, machinists, tool and die makers and other skilled trades. The remaining quarter are clerical, professional, technical, sales and managerial employees. Most of the semiskilled plant workers make automobile parts, assemble them into complete vehicles and put finishing touches on them. One of the largest occupations is machine tool operator. Many plant workers learn their jobs in a day or two. The industry looks for high school graduates who can perform routine work at a steady and fast pace. Manufacturers, because of the great stress placed upon design, maintenance and technological improvements, offer extensive training and apprenticeship programs. Employment in the industry is expected to increase somewhat over the next decade, but mostly in the clerical, sales and technical field. Automobile production will increase during the period, but mechanization and automation are expected to increase the production per employee. Thus, little increase is expected among the semi-skilled workers.

The petroleum and refining industry employs about 420,000 workers. This is divided into about 267,000 wage and salary workers in petroleum production and 153,000 in oil refining. About 80 per cent of the refinery workers are employed in only eight states: Texas, California, Pennsylvania, New York, Louisiana, Indiana, Illinois and New Jersey. Employment is expected to continue the decline which began in the 1950s, despite the greater demand for petroleum products. The decline will be felt most among the less skilled workers.

The pulp, paper and paper products industry employs about 710,000 workers. About 50 per cent of the workers are employed in mills that make pulp, paper or paperboard. The remaining workers are divided among plants that make paperboard boxes and other containers and those that produce a variety of other paper products. Women compose about one-fifth of the work force. Paper and pulp companies generally hire high school graduates, who start as laborers and helpers and advance to skilled jobs. Maintenance men are generally trained in the plants. Over-all employment in the industry is expected to increase, but again not in the less skilled production jobs. These should remain about the same or decline slightly.

About 1,250,000 people are employed by private industry and the Federal Government in America's "aerospace industry" making aircraft, missiles and space craft. About 55 per cent of all workers are employed in plant shops. The major job classifications are sheet metal work, machining and tool making, metal processing, assembly and installation, inspecting and testing, flight checkout, materials handling and maintenance. Those who perform these jobs receive a wide range of training, ranging from a few days to several years of on-the-job experience. Many of the jobs are highly expert and most interesting. To fill their needs for skilled workmen, most manufacturers have highly developed training programs offering abundant opportunities for unskilled high school graduates to learn most useful skills. Employment fluctuations can be very great within individual companies. The Department of Defense is the prime customer for the industry, and therefore its employment outlook depends greatly on foreign affairs and the arms race. Employment in the industry is expected to be static throughout the 1980s.

The apparel industry is the nation's largest employer of women in manufacturing; four-fifths of the 1.4 million workers are women. The principal job is sewing machine operator. Men predominate as cutters and markers. Opportunities appear excellent, both because the over-all employment is expected to rise and because the turnover rate among women employees is quite high. The high percentage of older women in the industry at present will create additional jobs for young women. The greatest need will be for sewing machine operators. Automation is expected to have little effect on the industry. Some previous training in sewing operations is preferred, but many plants hire workers who have had no experience and train them on the job. Pay is usually on the piecework basis. There is little opportunity for promotion beyond section forelady, although seamstresses have worked their way up to become production managers.

The making of bakery products such as bread and pastries employs about 282,000 men and women, with another 100,000 working in the retail bakeries. Most bakeries are small. Nearly half have fewer than ten employees. About 55 per cent of those employed in the perishable bakery products industry are in plant production. Most inexperienced production workers are hired as helpers. They wash and grease pans, carry ingredients to mixing machines and otherwise assist bakers. By working alongside skilled bakers, helpers are able to learn their trade. Some bakeries also have formal apprentice training programs. The consumption of bakery products is expected to increase, but the employment of less skilled people is likely to decline because of the increased mechanization of the industry.

The electric light and power industry employs about 495,000 workers. Private firms making electricity employ about 425,000. Federal, state and municipal government systems employ about 75,000. Many different levels of skills are used in the industry. Some 10 per cent of the employees are in occupations directly related to generating electricity. About 20 per cent are involved in the transmission and distribution of power. Another 20 per cent are in maintenance and repair. The remainder are in administrative, clerical and customer service, engineering, scientific and technical occupations. Power plant workers usually begin as cleanup men, then advance to helper and on to more skilled positions. It takes one to three years to become an auxiliary equipment operator and four to eight years to become a boiler, turbine or switchboard operator. There will be only several hundred openings a year for power plant operators, despite the increased production. The largest single category of worker in the transmission occupations is the lineman. It usually takes four years to become a skilled lineman. Inexperienced men are apprentices or are taught on the job, starting as groundmen and progressing to more difficult work. Much longer periods are needed to become substation operators and load dispatchers. Some increase in employment is expected. Other opportunities in the industry are as meter readers, who are usually inexperienced men, and metermen, who are skilled workers who install, test, maintain and repair meters in customers' premises. Metermen usually begin as helpers. About four years of on-the-job training is necessary.

These brief summaries of key industries indicate that there are still opportunities for unskilled production workers. But the opportunities are declining. At the same time, need for skilled workers is increasing.

Chapter 8

Training for Clerical Careers

In sixteen years of formal schooling the single most valuable course I took was a year of typing in high school. It changed my whole life. In college, when I decided to be a writer, typing was a necessary occupational skill. When I went into the Army, I discovered that almost the first question asked was "can you type?" The skill led to my assignment to Troop Information and Education, where I prepared (mostly by typing stencils) a front-line regimental newspaper in Korea. This work led to an interest in journalism, and my career as a newspaperman was enhanced certainly by my ability to type rapidly and effortlessly. For me, as for many others, journalism provided a training ground for a career as a writer of books such as this one.

It would be an oversimplification to say that typing makes a person a writer—or anything else—but typing is a skill useful in nearly every walk of life. It virtually guarantees employment, since business, industry, government, military services, hospitals, universities and every other institution sail on a sea of paper. Records, reports, correspondence, bills and thousands of other items all have to be typed, and the person who can type will never be long out of a job. Executives find it handy to be able to type a few sentences when they need to, as do doctors, lawyers, engineers and school teachers.

So I urge you, boys as well as girls, learn to type, if only a little. If you can't enroll in a regular typing class in junior or senior high school, find an old manual and a battered machine and teach yourself. It really isn't very difficult. Only patience and practice is required. Try to learn the so-called touch system, wherein you can type without looking at the keyboard. Better yet, practice until you can compose at the typewriter and are no longer restricted to copying material. But if all you are ever going to do is the old, two-fingered "hunt and peck" system, by all means learn that. I've seen people type 60 words a minute with two well-informed fingers.

Have you ever stopped to think about the changes the typewriter has caused in American life? Before the typewriter was invented, all records were written by hand. A fine, legible "hand" was an important career asset and hundreds of thousands of men (women didn't work much in those days) spent their entire lives copying records into ledgers. It must have been pure drudgery. The typewriter provided employment for millions, and marked the entrance of large numbers of women into the field. The ease with which legible copies could be made greatly increased the flow of business correspondence and in a way led to the communications industry, as well as enhancing business activity. A great many related clerical skills were fostered, and handwriting went into a decline. Just try to think of five occupations today in which the ability to handwrite legibly is important.

And the end is not in sight. The projection that over 17 million men and women will be employed in the clerical occupations by 1980 has already been reported. No one can foresee any decline in employment levels. Public education —and this is certainly one of the revolutionary changes wrought by the typewriter—is geared to training a seemingly unending stream of high school graduates trained in clerical skills. All of them obtain jobs, yet a shortage of employable people remains.

Seventy per cent of all clerical employees are women, but in the most common occupations, such as typing and stenography, 95 per cent of those employed are women. While many such jobs offer little opportunity for advancement, in part due to the continuing prejudice against the promotion of women to top-level positions, the battle against such discrimination is easing the situation somewhat, and the picture undoubtedly will continue to improve in the years to come. For the talented, determined woman, a secretarial position can lead to the executive suite.

Top confidential secretaries to high-ranking executives or professional men earn as much as $25,000 a year. More than money, such individuals earn status and responsibility. Consider the secretary of a top-ranking Federal executive in charge of a major governmental program. She plays an important role in running the entire program. She has the ear of the director, arranges his appointments and schedule. Her suggestions are important as he decides whom he wishes to see in the course of a day. In arranging his schedule, she funnels work to others in the agency. In these and a score of other unofficial ways she "runs" the agency. In tens of thousands of offices the "boss' secretary" is almost as important as the boss himself.

Secretaries and other clerical personnel who show leadership and executive ability tend to become administrative assistants, then move into other executive programs. The president of a large and famous New York publishing house was formerly secretary to the founder and principal owner. I have believed for many years that young men make a mistake in leaving clerical careers to the distaff side. Many business and industrial firms are looking for young men to be stenographers and secretaries. It offers a unique opportunity to learn a business from the ground up and move into administration and executive positions.

The largest clerical specialty group is stenographer-secretary. Nearly three million are employed. The principal skills are ability to type and take some form of shorthand dictation, but in actuality a great deal more is required. To be a secretary, a person must know the correct forms for a variety of business communications, telephone procedures, office practices, filing. The secretary must be pleasant, well organized, patient, hardworking, personable, tactful.

In large firms, a young person begins as a stenographer, often as a member of a "pool" of "stenos," taking dictation from several executives who do not rank a secretary or have more work than their secretary can handle. After taking the dictation, the stenographer types the materials into letters, memorandums, reports or whatever is appropriate.

Successful stenographers customarily become secretaries as openings become available, although some may be assigned as a stenographer under a secretary. The secretary works for one or two executives, generally handling clerical duties, phone calls, filing, schedules and other tasks the executives may require.

You must have special training to become a stenographer or secretary. The ability to type and take shorthand rapidly and accurately is absolutely essential. No one cares where you learned it, just so long as you have. You can learn it in high school, business schools, at home or in classes which many companies have established, but learn you must.

Many stenographers and secretaries specialize as law secretaries, court reporters and medical secretaries. Some become specialists in scientific, engineering and other technical fields or in hospital, university or institutional work. Some enhance their value by specializing in a particular manufacturing industry.

Half the stenographic skills are in demand, for there are more than 700,000 people (95 per cent women) employed as typists. The basic skill, typing, is the same, but it is applied in thousands of different ways. Beginning typists may type envelopes and headings on form letters or copy from handwritten or edited typewritten copy. More experienced or senior typists may work from rough drafts, type statistical or technical material, cut stencils and operate teletypewriters, proportional spacing typewriters or other more sophisticated equipment.

There are related specialties, such as typists who transcribe correspondence and other material from sound-dictating equipment. There are policy writers in insurance companies who type information onto insurance policy forms. Waybill clerks type billing information onto forms in transportation companies. Mortgage clerks perform similar functions in financial institutions.

Typing is often combined with other clerical skills. Thus, there are receptionists who handle the switchboard, greet customers and also serve as typists. There are clerk-typists who perform a variety of filing, routing, billing and other functions in addition to typing. But whatever the job, the ability to type is the core of the occupation.

Bookkeeping workers form another large clerical occupational group. More than 1,340,000, 90 per cent of them women, are so employed, the Department of Labor estimates. Again the tasks need little explanation. Bookkeepers maintain the accounts of business firms in journals, ledgers and other forms. They maintain records of receipts and expenditures under direction of an accountant or head bookkeeper. Generally speaking, they are "hand" book-keepers—that is, they handwrite sums into ledgers—but most also use adding, calculating and bookkeeping machines. Some typing skill is often required, along with knowledge of business arithmetic and bookkeeping.

The opportunities in this occupation are less than in other clerical specialties. Mechanization and automation will continue to diminish the need for bookkeepers. Bookkeeping, tabulating, mailing and a variety of other business machines are being used to replace old-fashioned hand records. Now, as we have seen, a new revolution is brewing with teleprocessing equipment, which will link branch office equipment to centralized computers. But these trends do not mean that the bookkeeping occupation will disappear. There will always be a need for it, but there will be less of a need for people to do routine tasks.

In recent years office machinery operation has been one of the fastest-growing clerical specialties, with 365,000, three-quarters of them women, employed. Among the major office machines are billing machines, which register credits and debits on bills which go to customers; adding and calculating machines, which are either manually or electrically operated, to add, subtract, multiply, divide and make other computations in preparing payrolls, invoices and statistical summaries; mailing equipment, which manually or electrically addresses, seals, stamps and bundles large amounts of bills, circulars, magazines and other correspondence; tabulating machines, which code information onto cards or other forms, sorts and files them and then reprocesses the information into any statistical form desired; duplicating machines, such as mimeograph or photocopying machines, which reproduce copies of documents for later dissemination.

The increasing use of such equipment indicates continued high employment in these areas for the next several years. Increased use of electronic teleprocessing equipment, which might cause a decline in the number of office machine operators, is being more than offset by the new, more sophisticated types of machines which are marketed. The teleprocessing equipment has led to the employment of 200,000 people to operate it. Extremely rapid growth is anticipated.

Another large clerical specialty is cashier, who accepts money from sales, makes change and records the transaction on cash registers, some of which also perform bookkeeping functions. There are 850,000 cashiers who work in stores, supermarkets, restaurants, theaters, industry and just about everywhere else money changes hands. Tens of thousands of jobs will be available annually in the foreseeable future.

One of the clerical specialties where men predominate is shipping and receiving clerking. Nearly 380,000 are employed, mostly in manufacturing and wholesale firms. But jobs are not customarily performed by the same person. The shipping clerk sees that orders are correctly filled. He types or prepares bills of lading and other shipping forms. The receiving clerk reverses the process, seeing that the proper orders have been received and that the invoice is complete and correct. He may process claims and search for lost shipments, as well as reroute merchandise to the proper department or warehouse. Some mechanization and streamlining seems likely in warehousing operations, but many thousands of jobs will be available annually. Clerks have excellent advancement opportunities into warehouse management and production control.

The clerical specialties offer great opportunity for high school graduates. With the exception of typing, shorthand and bookkeeping, clerical skills can be learned on the job.

Many young people launch their clerical careers after high school with no training in typing, shorthand and business practices. They begin as messengers, receptionists and file clerks, or they are taught to operate duplicating machines, cash registers and other business equipment.

Modern business machines are complex devices, but they are quite simple to operate. A high school graduate can be taught to perform simple repetitive calculations in just a few minutes. Mercantile concerns routinely train business machine operators. R. H. Macy and Company, a New York department store, for example, employs about a thousand young people who have no previous experience and trains them to operate machines which record all of the millions of sales transactions conducted by the firm each year. Cash receipts, billing, credits, orders and all manner of statistical summaries are processed by these young people. It is, admittedly, repetitive work. There is close supervision during the learning period, but employees gradually become expert business machine operators. Not only stores, but every business and industry that has a large accounting, bookkeeping and billing operation trains its own equipment operators.

There is, to give other examples, no particular secret to operating keypunch machines or mimeograph or photocopying equipment. Not more than a day or two of on-the-job instruction is needed to give a person competence in at least routine tasks. Filing can be complex, but a person can learn it on the job. Mailing operations, shipping and receiving are taught routinely by employers.

It is true that simple clerical jobs offer little career advancement—if that is all the skills a person learns. If you are interested in a clerical career, but left school without stenographic or bookkeeping training, the simpler clerical tasks offer you an opportunity to receive training. You first learn simple tasks, then more complex ones. If you enroll in night business courses, you can easily add the valuable stenographic, accounting and other skills.

Opportunities are available in every city and town in the country, for the need for clerical skills is universal. As you know, clerical employees usually work regular hours in pleasant surroundings. The work, while demanding, is often interesting and satisfying. These factors, as well as the status of clerical workers, the career advancement and the consistently high levels of employment surely explain why 13 million people work in these occupations and why you should take advantage of the training opportunities offered to you.

Chapter 9

Training for a Career in Sales

Another of the great areas of opportunity for the high school graduate is in sales—all types of sales, involving hundreds of thousands of different products. There are, according to government estimates, about 4.9 million salesmen in the United States, and most of them have no more than a high school education.

The greatest opportunity for both training and careers is in retail sales (including supermarkets) and wholesale selling. Certain industrial firms, particularly those in the technological fields, customarily seek college graduates, particularly those who have a scientific, engineering or mercantile background. This may be the rule, but there are many exceptions. The qualified high school graduate should not consider any field closed to him. Other selling specialties, such as insurance, real estate, stocks and bonds, while open to the high school graduate are not usually available until he is a few years older and has had some experience in other types of sales.

Department stores and other retail establishments employ about two and a half million salesclerks, a little more than half of them women. There are tens of thousands of openings every year all over the country. Employers want high school graduates who have ability to make simple calculations, can learn to operate cash registers, are interested in the products they will sell and have engaging personalities.

Department stores have efficient machinery for training salesclerks. After a preliminary orientation, the clerks attend a few classes in which they learn how to write a sales slip, record credit and cash sales on the cash register, interpret the store's price marking system, order and reorder merchandise when necessary and become familiar with store policies and practices. Training then continues on the job under the supervision of experienced salesclerks.

The inexperienced clerk usually begins in such departments as hosiery, housewares, hardware, toys, gloves, costume jewelry and candy, which require less salesmanship. In these departments customers are more apt to select their own merchandise and present it to the salesclerk to record the sale, or the merchandise comes in prepackaged sizes and colors so that the salesclerk needs less information about the product.

With experience and upon demonstrating sales ability, the salesclerk progresses to departments where more knowledge of the product and sales ability is required. In clothing, for example, the clerk will need to advise the customer about fit and fashion and be familiar with such matters as the washability and wearability of the garment. A person selling sports equipment will need to know the use of the product and be familiar with sports. In furniture, he will need to know the construction, upholstery and cleanability and have some knowledge of interior decoration to persuade the customer to buy the product.

The top selling jobs are those which pay a commission to the salesclerk. Women frequently earn commissions—that is, a small percentage of the dollar volume of their sales— in the departments selling fashion merchandise. Some

A group of on the job trainees at Clairton Works visit a product flow panel board area for instruction on this phase of plant's operation.

These trainees are conferring on a joint report they have been assigned to work out for a product presentation.

Members of an on the job training group are calibrating an optical
pyrometer which they have cleaned and repaired.

The instructor is demonstrating the techniques used in trouble shooting
high production vacuum systems.

Courtesy A.T.&T.Co.
Bell craftsmen study the circuitry of a telephone system that provides
various features for the convenience of business customers.

Courtesy United States Steel Corporation
To assure that skills keep pace with rapidly changing technological
advances, Clairton Works on-the-job trainees get programmed
instruction from teaching machines.

Courtesy A. T. & T. Co.
Instructor makes point to commercial representatives trainees on use of handbook containing day-to-day reference material, in classroom training.

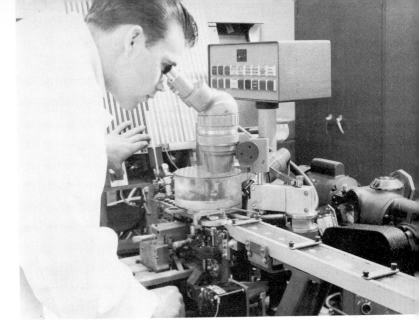

Courtesy International Business Machines Corporation
Solid Logic Technology circuit modules—the basic electronic building
blocks of IBM System/360 Computers—are manufactured by highly
mechanized machinery. This machine uses a rotary "squeegee"
to force metallic ink through a patterned mesh screen, producing
the circuit network on the substrate.

Courtesy International Business Machines Corporation
Employee checks Solid Logic Technology substrates after resistors
have been screen-printed onto the substrates.

Amid the fast paced activity
of the business office, a
supervisor discusses a
customer's problems with a
representative.

A check on the record of
the "print out" which is the
end of a job on the 1401
machine, located at the Data
Process Center, Varick
Street, New York.

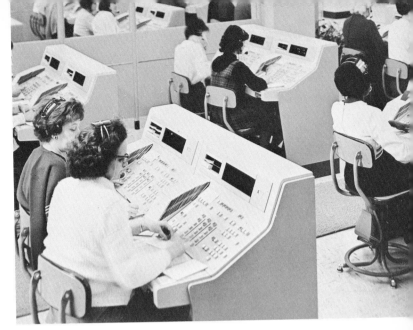

Courtesy A.T.&T.Co.

Operators at TSP Consoles—new pushbutton consoles to help customers get much faster service on person-to-person calls, coin telephones and others that need operator assistance.

Courtesy A.T.&T.Co.

The new decorator-styled Trimline telephone now being offered in many states.

Courtesy A. T. & T. Co.
More than 2,000 Traffic Service Positions like these in Philadelphia
are now in use. They make possible faster service on person-to-person
and credit card calls, and when charges are reversed.

Courtesy A. T. & T. Co.
More than sixty thousand
users of teletypewriter ex-
change service can now make
connections three times faster by dialing directly through
nationwide network.

women's wear specialty shops have only commission sales-clerks. For men, top commission items are household appliances, television and hi-fi equipment.

Commission salesmen, whether in a department store or specialty shop, usually earn· $10,000 to $20,000 a year. These positions are greatly sought after, and they usually go to the senior and most able salesclerks who have a proven record of sales ability. But these jobs are available to young people who may have started at little more than the minimum wage, but learned their skills while on the job.

Most retail salesclerks discover in a few weeks whether they like to sell. Those who remain are usually quite enthusiastic about their work. They discover the products in which they are interested and then specialize in selling them. Women who sell fashion items, for example, have a great interest in apparel. It should not be surprising that book salesmen read a lot or that salesmen of power tools are do-it-yourselfers or that salesmen of sporting equipment play golf or fish every chance they get. There are busy, hectic days in every store, but most salesclerks enjoy their work, the hours, the stimulation and the variety of the customers. Some salesclerks remain with one department store all of their working lives, for many of our great department stores are institutions which look upon their employees as "part of the family." Other salesclerks change jobs until they find the position that is right for them, perhaps advancing into wholesale selling.

Few other occupations offer the opportunity for training and advancement to high-paying jobs that selling does. In the retail field, there is great opportunity to become a manager. A common first promotion for the able salesclerk is to sales manager, who supervises all the selling activities in a department. The sales manager trains and assigns personnel, and he sees that merchandise is displayed and marked properly and that customers receive good service. Above the sales manager is the group manager, who supervises several departments, and the merchandise manager, who has charge of sales throughout the whole store. It is also possible for able salesclerks to become buyers. These are men and women who purchase the goods which the store later sells to its customers. The buyer purchases from wholesalers and manufacturers, both in this country and abroad. Admittedly, buyers are commonly groomed through the store's programs for college graduates, but if a clerk shows the ability, there is nothing to bar him from a career as a buyer.

There are many other career opportunities in a department store. People with artistic inclination can go into display, sales promotion, publicity and advertising. There are careers in the receiving and warehousing operations. The merchandise, ordered by the buyers, is delivered to the store and its various warehouses. There the order has to be checked, the parcels counted and sorted, the price marked. Then the merchandise is routed and delivered to the proper warehouses and storerooms. All of these are separate operations, and high school graduates perform them. Jobs as checkers, sorters, markers and stockmen offer a chance to learn warehousing and merchandise handling and lead to supervisory positions. People working in materials handling can also transfer to sales and other departments.

The opportunities for training and advancement which are offered in a large department store diminish somewhat in a smaller store. The proprietor of the store or the manager tends to act as buyer, sales manager and warehouse manager, yet selling in a specialty shop can be financially rewarding, particularly on a commission basis.

All of you reading this book will be familiar with at least some of the jobs in a supermarket, but what you may not realize is that these are not simply jobs, but training opportunities leading to careers in food retailing.

A modern supermarket, particularly those operated by a large chain, is really four stores in one. There is a manager, and under him are four department heads, the grocery manager, produce manager, meat manager and cash department head, who supervises the cashiers, checkout and bundling of purchases for the customer.

The most important department is groceries, which includes all items other than meat and produce. Over 65 per cent of a typical supermarket's gross sales are of canned and frozen foods, bulk items, soaps, paper products, dairy items, bread and pastries and hundreds of other items. Under the grocery manager are two assistant managers and a number of clerks.

The produce department, as you know, includes fresh fruits and vegetables and accounts for about 9 per cent of the gross sales. There is a head produce clerk and several clerks. The meat department usually does about 25 per cent of the gross business. There are head meatcutter, journeymen and apprentice meatcutters and wrappers employed in the department. The cash department includes the cashiers who record the sales and the bundlers who place the customer's purchases in bags and sometimes carry them to her car.

Traditionally one begins as a clerk, obtaining the job by contacting the store manager. There is an interview and perhaps some simple tests. The grocery clerk receives material in the stock room, opens cartons, marks prices, loads shelves, helps to maintain the store and its inventory and assists at the cash registers during busy periods. The produce clerk performs essentially the same duties, except that he must protect the more perishable items in his department, rotating items frequently, picking out spoiled produce and keeping the remainder iced down. There is some packaging of fruits and vegetables in plastic bags.

This is hard work and not very stimulating, although there is plenty of room for responsibility and initiative. But the young man who shows leadership and potential has a bright future. We have seen the promotional opportunities to head clerk, assistant department manager, department manager and store manager. Beyond that are many managerial positions in buying, warehousing, product manufacture, pricing, advertising, district managing and others too numerous to mention here. The point is that the young man who starts out stacking cans is not just filling a job but launching a career. As in so many industries, supermarket executives believe their business is best learned from the bottom up, by loading shelves and marking cans before assuming supervision over others who do the same tasks. And the retail food industry is growing so rapidly that promotional opportunities will be excellent for many years.

The meat department offers a chance to learn a marketable skill. Starting as a wrapper, helper or apprentice, a young person can learn to be a meatcutter through on-the-job training. Cutting sides of meat into steaks, chops, roasts and other forms requires expertise that is in demand. Working in a supermarket offers an opportunity to learn it.

There are many types of retail selling positions for which the young man or woman with desire and ambition can be trained. House-to-house selling is perhaps the oldest form of sales, yet it is booming as never before, with more than 1,500 firms marketing their products in this manner. Selling house to house offers great advantages to the manufacturer, because it enables the customer to see the product in his own home and try it himself. For elderly people and shut-ins the house-to-house salesman performs a most important function.

The major firms of this industry, such as Avon Products and Fuller Brush, offer sales training programs to prospective salesmen. While earnings may be small in the beginning, eventually the person with aptitude and energy earns a significant salary, for commissions are usually 25 or 30 per cent of the price of the merchandise. One of the appeals of house-to-house work is that the salesman is essentially an independent businessman, for he purchases the goods from the manufacturer, then works as hard as he wishes to sell them.

The automotive salesman is another retail salesman because he deals directly with the consumer. His products are new and used cars and trucks, parts and accessories, or service on vehicles. Automotive selling requires considerable expertise and a high level of salesmanship. Cars cost between $2,000 and $10,000, and the customer does not make such a purchase casually. Moreover, the American motorist is well informed about engines, performance and other aspects of automotive technology. He expects the salesman to be well informed and able to answer detailed questions about the car quickly and accurately. Finally, the automobile industry is highly competitive. There is always a dealer down the street endeavoring to sell a similar car and often the same one.

For these reasons, dealers look for salesmen who have both expertise and sales ability. While many young men are employed, some experience in the automotive field is required. Men have gone into automotive sales after working as a gas station attendant, mechanic or helper in a garage, preferably the dealer's own service department. Training is usually informal. The manufacturers provide manuals and some training classes, but for the most part the salesman learns from experienced men and through his own efforts. The new man may begin selling used cars and trucks before graduating to the new car field.

Careers selling real estate, insurance and, to a lesser extent, stocks and bonds are open to high school graduates, but in frankness it must be said they are seldom open to eighteen-year-olds. Maturity and stability are important assets in these positions. An insurance agent, for example, helps a customer plan his entire estate, going over the customer's income and financial obligations. Insurance companies feel that agents should have their own feet on the ground before advising others in these matters.

Another reason for insisting on maturity is that these types of selling require a high level of self-discipline. The real estate or insurance agent has some supervision, but he must be a "self-starter." He has no time clock to punch, no one looking over his shoulder to witness how hard he works. Rather, he must be motivated, dedicated and responsible enough to do his job largely on his own. Too, these selling specialties, while highly lucrative for the man who has aptitude and persistence, have lean periods at the outset. An insurance agent's earnings may be quite small for a couple of years until he builds his clientele and becomes established. Insurance and real estate firms feel, rightly or wrongly, that recent high school graduates lack the needed "staying power."

But a young person interested in insurance, real estate and securities sales can prepare for these careers. He can perhaps find a nonselling clerical position in an office, or sell part time while working at other jobs.

The wholesale salesman calls upon stores, selling the products of a single manufacturer or a group of them. Most companies have training programs for wholesale salesmen, some of which last for two years, but recent high school graduates cannot qualify for all of them. Some employers demand expertise obtainable only in college. Still other employers seek sales experience and that elusive maturity.

The wholesale salesman usually covers a territory, often a geographically large one, calling on stores, offices and accounts throughout it. Since territories are assigned on the basis of seniority or sales performance, the beginning salesman usually receives the less compact territory. He frequently has to travel and spend considerable time away from home—another reason employers want mature, stable men. Some companies place sales trainees in departments which process reorders and perform other services for established customers, before assigning them to a territory.

To sum up, the high school graduate can qualify in the wholesale field, but he ought to gain some experience elsewhere in preparation for it. The same is true of industrial salesmen. They work for manufacturers whose customers are other manufacturers buying raw materials, machinery, components, packaging and other products and supplies. Most industrial selling demands a high level of expertise, not only about the products being sold but about the use the customer is going to make of it. No high school graduate would have this expertise, but he could achieve it by working in the industry. Those individuals who take advantage of other training opportunities to become technicians, for example, could certainly aspire to industrial sales careers.

Selling is one of the most rewarding careers and with the exceptions that have been noted, it is the province of the high school graduate. Those who have the personality and inclination for sales find it stimulating and exciting work. It offers great variety to those who truly enjoy meeting people. There is the challenge of making the sale and a feeling of service in helping a customer make sound, useful purchases. Selling has a high independence quotient in that the salesman is largely on his own, making a success of himself on his own efforts. There is a ready yardstick of his abilities too: how many sales he makes and how much he earns in commissions. Most experienced, able people in sales wouldn't consider doing any other type of work.

Sales is also one of the truly high-paying careers open to high school graduates. Top wholesale salesmen and people in real estate and stocks and bonds make over $200,000 a year. Many men in industrial, wholesale, and certain commission retail selling positions earn more than $25,000 a year. But the young person invariably starts at a rather low salary. His earnings and commissions keep pace with his experience and selling ability. Perhaps more than in any other profession, success in sales depends on the individual. He becomes what he makes of himself.

Selling is perhaps not for the person who likes the security of a regular paycheck and lacks competitive drive or relishes his independence. For those who do like selling, the employment outlook is excellent. Our economy is turning out more products constantly, all of which need to be sold. There will always be an opportunity for salesmen.

Chapter 10

Training in Transportation

The United States is a nation on the move. At any given moment, one-fifth of our population is transferring its place of residence, across the street or across the nation. In a recent year 900 million people traveled by airplane, bus or train for a total distance of nearly 100 billion passenger miles, a figure computed by multiplying the number of passengers times the miles they traveled. Then there are the products and materials we ship by public transportation—three billion tons in a recent year. When figured in ton miles (one ton carried one mile) the transportation industries recorded 1.5 trillion ton miles in moving America's products. The industries transported everything from a tiny transistor chip made at East Fishkill, New York, to a giant Saturn rocket needed at Cape Kennedy, a newly hatched chick to minerals which have rested beneath the earth for millions of years.

Our American society depends upon transportation. Without it, we would still be an agrarian nation, living on farms and restricted to those goods which we could produce ourselves. In a modern industrial nation, transportation is its lifeblood. The prosperity of a nation is in direct proportion to the efficiency of its transportation. Thus, there can be few more important and rewarding careers than in transportation.

High school graduates searching for training should definitely look to the transportation industries. There is a trend in the airline, bus, train, truck and inland-waterways industries to employ more scientific, technical and other college-educated persons, but the high school graduate seems likely to remain the backbone of these industries. There is a simple, logical reason for this. Transportation involves performance. There are trucks and buses to drive, passengers to ticket and be made comfortable, bills and invoices to be processed, shipments to be protected and warehoused. There is no particular theory involved in any of it. One doesn't learn how to correctly balance the load in a truck trailer from a book. He learns it by experience.

There is another reason why high school graduates are sought in transportation. All of these industries value personality highly. Drivers, for example, must be mature, stable men, quick of reflex, slow of temper, without any "hot rod" tendencies in them. The airlines annually hire thousands of young men and women who are pleasant and personable and who genuinely like people and enjoy helping them. Education does not particularly develop these qualities. A person either has them, or he does not.

Men and women in transportation usually stand apart from their fellow man. Theirs is a fast-moving, sometimes hectic business. They are on the go and they are "doing things." They are behind the wheel of big vehicles, moving mountains of cargo and speeding people and goods to distant places. There is a wanderlust to transportation workers. They cannot sit still, and they take risks, for there is an element of danger to many of the transportation jobs, despite the great emphasis on safety. Nearly every transportation worker will tell you his job "gets in the blood." He is frequently highly paid, but that is not why he does it.

He is so in love with his work that he really couldn't consider doing anything else.

If you are interested in a career in transportation, there are many opportunities available for training. Let's consider some of the major opportunities characteristic of each industry. Some opportunities will be obvious and will not be covered here. For example, all transportation companies employ clerical help, which was discussed in Chapter 8.

Commercial airlines have long been the most glamorous part of the transportation industry. But in the 1970s, a bit of the sheen has been rubbed off by hard times and a few economic realities. Airline passenger traffic continues to rise, but at perhaps half the former rate of 15 per cent growth a year. Airline profits are generally way down. This has been caused by extremely expensive purchases of new aircraft such as the Boeing 747 and generally high wage contracts negotiated years ago when times were prosperous. Now airlines are in a cost squeeze. Many of the luxury frills have been trimmed and most airlines have laid off personnel. There will be growth in commercial aviation in the 1970s and many job opportunities, but the extravagant forecasts of the 1960s now seem pie-in-the-sky.

The airline pilot is the most glamorous transportation employee. Senior jet pilots now earn about $50,000 a year for flying about 80 hours a month in the huge 300-passenger Boeing 747 jets. These wages are paid because of the skill required of the pilot and the responsibility he assumes. The earnings are computed on the basis of the speed and weight of the plane and the distance flown.

The practice may change, but at present, airlines do not train pilots. To become a pilot, you must have a pilot's license and some flying experience before you are hired. A college education is desired, but it is not mandatory. You can obtain your flying skills at a flying school, but the military services remain the principal source of training. After you are hired by an airline, you receive constant training. You begin as a copilot on the smallest, slowest planes (piston-engine craft when they are still used), then progress to turboprop planes, small jets (727s) and then to larger jets. With experience as a copilot, you are promoted to pilot or captain, again starting with the smallest, slowest equipment and progressing as before. Seniority is dominant among pilots, determining promotions, equipment flown and route assignments.

The Department of Labor was predicting in 1972 that a rapid increase in the number of pilots employed would occur throughout the decade. Perhaps, but this contrasts with the fact that in 1972, commercial airlines still had not hired back all of their pilots previously laid off. The prediction perhaps rests more on the growing importance of non-scheduled and charter air service flying groups of vacationers to resorts and other spas. And, of course, the demand for pilots reflects the need for other operating and ground employees.

The airline stewardess is the most celebrated operating person next to the pilot. Qualifications vary, but in general the applicant must be twenty years old. Her height must be between five feet two inches and five feet nine inches, and she must weigh between 105 and 140 pounds, in proportion to her height. A high school education and some business experience is qualifying, but airlines prefer some college background or training in nursing.

With these rather simple qualifications, airlines have no shortage of applicants, yet they have difficulty finding the right girls. Only one out of every thirty-five applicants is accepted, because the airlines are looking for a rather special girl. She should be comely and have a slender figure, yet not be dependent upon a lot of makeup to appear attractive. More importantly, the applicant should not be overly conscious of her attractiveness. Airlines want the "girl next door" type who has a warm, friendly, outgoing personality. She should be poised, extremely patient and most forbearing. And she must be well organized, able to perform tasks in a great hurry while seeming not to.

Some of the stewardess' tasks will show why these qualities are vital. She may serve a four-course dinner to forty or fifty people during an hour's flight, while answering questions, distributing magazines, warming babies' bottles, giving instructions on how to inflate a life jacket in case of emergency, hanging overcoats and advising passengers about connecting flights. All the while, she is expected to smile, smile, smile. She must not become ruffled, annoyed or discourteous.

The capacity to perform in such a manner resides deep within a person and is enhanced by training. If you are selected as a stewardess, you will attend a school at which you learn about airplanes, flying, ticketing, seating passengers and emergency procedures. You'll receive courses in preparing and serving meals and cocktails. There is a charm course in which you learn to improve your walking and talking, maintain good posture, move gracefully, fix your hair and apply makeup. You'll be instructed in techniques for dealing with the angry and impatient passenger and the anxious one. It amounts to training in being a good hostess that will be useful to you all your life.

It is virtually axiomatic in the aviation industry that there is a shortage of stewardesses. There are many opportunities for jobs and the Department of Labor predicts a "rapid" growth throughout the 1970s. But the growth is tempered by several developments, including the extension of the age limit for stewardesses beyond age 32, the policy of airlines to continue to employ stewardesses after marriage and the hiring of more males as stewards. The opportunities for young women are still there, but the competition is keener.

There are several positions in airline terminal operations for which high school graduates are sought. One is reservations agent, young men and women who handle the requests for reservations which come in over the phone. Every airline employs thousands of young people who have good diction, pleasant voices and agreeable personalities. They answer questions, quote fares, give arrival and departure times and advise about connecting flights, then make the reservation. The reservations agent works behind the scenes and is seldom seen by the public. He or she wears street clothes. Shift work is usually required.

The first promotion for the able reservations agent is to ticket agent, the young man or woman seen in uniform behind the airline ticket counter. He greets passengers, sells or validates tickets, provides travel information, weighs luggage and performs other duties. Again, airlines are looking for the attractive, personable young person. Some shift work is required.

A related job is PSR—passenger service representative. This is the young woman in uniform who greets passengers in front of the ticket counter. She answers questions and guides passengers to counters, gates and other terminal facilities. The PSR invariably has an incredibly agreeable personality. She greets thousands of people in the course of a work day and is expected to be truly delighted to see every one of them.

Airlines train thousands of reservations agents, ticket agents and PSRs every year. Airline growth causes a high demand, and there is a high turnover of personnel. The women are young and eligible for marriage, and the shift work is undesirable to many people. Training customarily occurs in classes at which ticketing and related procedures are taught, then in on-the-job training.

These positions all have career potential. A young person can advance to supervisor, to ticket manager and into terminal management. A person can go into sales—that is, calling on travel agents and large airline customers. He can go into personnel, airport operations, training and many other management positions.

The greatest opportunity for training toward a skilled, high-paid job in aviation is in aviation mechanics. More than 136,000 are now employed, 54,000 by the scheduled airlines and 52,000 in independent repair places. Another 20,500 are employed as civilians by the Air Force and over 10,000 by the Navy. Employment is expected to increase rapidly throughout the 1970s. The skills may be learned on-the-job. The young man begins as a plane refueler, perhaps, or as a helper. Airlines and other companies offer formal training courses to qualified applicants. Perhaps a better route of entry is to enroll in private aviation mechanic schools certified by the Federal Aviation Agency. Or, such courses may be taken coincident with on-the-job experience.

There are many other opportunities to learn a marketable skill in aviation. A person can begin as a baggage handler and make a career in terminal operations. There are opportunities for radio operators, meteorologists, computer programmers, teletypists and other communications workers, food service employees and others too numerous to mention. One of the more demanding, yet attractive careers is as an air traffic controller, all of whom are employed by the Federal Aviation Agency of the federal government.

All airline employees have travel privileges at reduced fares, which is one of the attractions of the industry.

There are opportunities to become a bus driver, but not for the recent high school graduate. The minimum age for most bus drivers is twenty-four years of age. He must be in good health and be able to pass a battery of aptitude and psychological tests.

The bus driver is a rather special individual. Having the reflexes and judgment to drive well is only the beginning. Bus companies expect their drivers to be exceptional men, able to drive for long periods in total safety. Defensive driving is the hallmark of the occupation. Bus drivers must not only have their own bus under control at all times, they must be constantly alert to any errors made by drivers of other vehicles and prepared to take evasive action. They must have a psychological makeup that will prohibit any wool gathering, risk taking or other unsafe driving practices. They must conform to a thick manual which sets forth rigid rules for driving. At the same time they must be pleasant to passengers. All of this adds up to maturity and stability. Rewards are high, with senior men earning more than $15,000 a year.

The large intercity carriers, such as Greyhound and Trailways, train many of their own drivers. The new driver is expected to be an excellent driver before he is hired and to have had some experience in driving trucks or other large vehicles. He then receives six to eight weeks of instruction, most of it driving over the company's routes to become familiar with terminals, schedules and procedures. As with airlines, route assignments are based on seniority. There are promotional opportunities for bus drivers, to dispatcher and supervisory positions, but these tend to pay less than top drivers earn. Thus, most drivers tend to remain drivers throughout their careers.

In bus terminal operations, the high school graduate customarily starts as a baggage clerk, who places outbound luggage in the bus and removes inbound luggage, either checking it or handing it to the passenger. He must become familiar with bus routes, destinations and methods of baggage handling. Training is on the job.

Other terminal employees are selected on a seniority basis from among the baggage handlers. The next step up is to telephone information clerk, who gives information about routes, fares and arrival and departure times in answer to telephone queries. The next promotion is to counter information clerk, who performs much the same tasks, but directly with the public in the terminal. In time, a clerk may be promoted to ticket agent, who sells tickets and trip insurance to passengers.

There are promotional opportunities into terminal management and even higher positions, although the trend now is to recruit college graduates as management trainees.

Mechanics may also learn their skills through bus companies. The practice is to start young men as cleaners, washers and janitors, then promote them to gasmen, greasers and utility men. Those who show ability become helpers to mechanics and eventually fully qualified mechanics.

American railroads are undergoing a metamorphosis. For a half century prior to 1920, trains were the dominant means of transportation in this country, but with the coming of cars and trucks, railroads went into a decline. Passenger volume dropped drastically and service was reduced. Freight volumes also declined. Employment went down sharply. But starting in the 1950s, the railroads began an upward trend. A series of mergers made the industry more efficient, and large sums were spent to modernize equipment with new diesel locomotives, an array of larger and more specialized freight cars and automatic switching equipment. Railroads have attracted back some of their lost business and have opened up new markets.

Operating crews are trained on the job. A young man begins as a brakeman or flagman on freight trains or baggageman or ticket collector on passenger trains. The latter two job titles are descriptive. A brakeman's basic job is to couple and uncouple air hoses on freight cars. The flagman stands behind the train when it is stopped and signals oncoming trains and the engineer of his own train to protect it from a rear-end collision. In practice there are many other duties.

Under union rules, brakemen, baggagemen and ticket collectors may be promoted to conductor on the basis of ability, fitness and seniority. The conductor, whether in passenger or freight service, has charge of the train and all other workmen on it. He is responsible for the safety and care of the train and the passengers or commodities it carries.

Traditionally the locomotive engineer began as a fireman, who stoked the fires in the steam engine in days gone by. In the era of diesels, the "fireman" has acted as assistant to the engineer. In recent years, there has been a trend to phase out the fireman. At this writing there is an oversupply of engineers and firemen trained to be engineers.

There are many other types of railroad operating positions that do not involve riding trains. There are about 90,000 (mostly men) employed in about thirty different job classifications. The young man starts as a clerk, clerk-telephoner or telegrapher. These lead to such positions as station agent, dispatcher, assistant trainmaster and trainmaster, who maintains the safe movement of traffic in terminals, in rail yards and over the road. These employees consult with shippers, control expenses, properly distribute empty freight cars and in general carry on the business of meeting the needs of customers. Another area of training is in rail yards, where trains are formed and broken down. Among the positions here are sidemen, switchmen and yardmasters.

Two other large areas of railroad employment should be mentioned. About 82,000 are employed in maintenance of track, right of track, right of way, bridges and other structures. Many of these are craft workers, such as carpenters, structural ironworkers and operating engineers. Young men without previous training can begin as laborers, helpers and apprentices.

About 150,000 work in railroad shops, where they build, remodel and repair railroad rolling stock. These vast shops, located in central cities all over the country, employ large numbers of blacksmiths, boilermakers, electrical workers, machinists, sheet metal workers, stationary engineers and other craftsmen. Railroad shops provide an opportunity to learn a marketable skill by starting as a laborer or apprentice and moving up to helper.

It is traditional in the railroad industry, perhaps more than in other transportation industries, to work up from the bottom. Top railroad management executives frequently hold union status as conductors, engineers, trainmasters or yardmasters. Many executives began as clerks in a freight terminal or a district or division office, learned the business and gradually accepted ever greater responsibility. Yet it must be said that the employment situation in the rail industry is not very bright. The decline in the number of operating employees which began in the 1950s is expected to continue in the 1970s. The Amtrak program of the federal government under which high speed passenger trains are to be built and operated may eventually reverse this trend, but not for several years. Railroading is simply not a career offering more than limited opportunity these days.

The trucking industry is the behemoth of the transportation industry. It claims to carry three-fourths the freight transported in this country, to use enough gasoline and other fuels to fill a convoy of tank trucks 20,000 miles long and enough tires to form three tire chains across the United States. There are nearly 18 million privately owned trucks in this country. And each year the industries buy nearly two million new trucks. The industry supports thirteen companies manufacturing trucks, 550 firms making truck and bus bodies, and another 170 companies manufacturing the trailers hauled by trucks.

There are 9 million men and women employed in the industry, including 2.4 million truck drivers. They operate a wide variety of vehicles from small pickup and panel trucks to huge over-the-road interstate transports. There are over 15,000 trucking firms in the United States (they operate more than 40 per cent of the world's trucks), but less than one-tenth of them gross one million dollars or more in revenues. The industry is composed predominately of small firms.

Truck driving is one of the largest single occupational groups, yet, strangely enough, the industry trains very few. Large companies have training courses in their methods of operations and in good safety practices, but they do not train a truck driver from scratch. There is nothing resembling an apprenticeship program.

Truck drivers are largely self-taught, although there are driver training schools which should be recommended. Drivers begin as automobile drivers, then transfer to smaller and then bigger trucks. Since large truck fleets insist upon some experience, most drivers begin by working for small firms, making deliveries around town or short "hauls" of steel, produce or other materials in the communities where they live. Two or three years of such experience, together with a good driving record, usually qualifies for employment in most firms.

There are several types of truck drivers, the most important of which are the over-the-road drivers. There are about 600,000 men employed to drive the large interstate tractor-trailers. The large fleet owners prefer men who are at least twenty-five years of age, who have had considerable driving experience and who indicate competence, maturity, good judgment and safety-consciousness. These men customarily drive the same route between terminals of a fleet owner. The terminals are spaced so that a driver going at legal speeds can make the run in ten hours, with an hour's stop for rest. His route is laid out, and he may not deviate from it without good reason. The trucks are equipped with devices which record his speed and any stops he makes, all of which must be accounted for. After laying over at the terminal, he returns with a load in the opposite direction.

Another type of driver makes pickups and deliveries of merchandise between the truck terminal and the company's customers in a community. In a city these drivers have to be expert at negotiating city traffic, but usually less driving experience is required than for over-the-road drivers. Local drivers, who form the largest group of truck drivers, all perform duties other than driving. They load and unload merchandise at customers' warehouses. They fill out invoices and other forms and sometimes collect payment for the goods. Despite the fact that the work involves more lifting, most drivers prefer this type of work. Their hours are regular, and it is more interesting in that they deal directly with the public.

Another large category of truck drivers are called "routemen," who work for nontrucking firms. They sell or deliver the company products. The milkman is an example of a routeman. These are rewarding jobs and a training ground for local and over-the-road drivers.

For every truck driver there are approximately three non-driving or terminal employees. A large group of these are freight handlers. As the name implies, they handle the shipment to and from the trucks, usually operating fork-lifts and other mobile equipment. A high school graduate often starts as a freight handler to become familiar with the sorting and movement of freight. If he shows initiative, he seldom stays a handler long, but moves into any of several positions. A dock foreman who supervises handlers is one. Or he can move into dispatching, where the assignment of trucks to make deliveries and pickups takes place. Most terminals have two-way radio contacts with the local drivers. Above the dispatcher is the terminal operations manager, who supervises all of the activities just described.

Another important terminal employee is the rating clerk, who figures both the route over which freight should be sent and the charges. This is a complex job, for there are thousands of different routes all of which have separate charges for various commodities. Yet the experienced rating clerk is expected to be both fast and accurate in quoting prices to customers. Rating clerks have learned a most marketable skill and are frequently among the highest-paid terminal employees. A young man usually trains on the job for several years before he becomes adept at this work.

Customer service is another important terminal activity. Here young men and women check on shipments which were not delivered in proper order. Some parcels may be lost or improper delivery may have occurred. Clerks check back to terminals which handled the shipment previously, retracing the merchandise.

The terminal also includes a number of accounting employees. There is a manifest clerk, who transcribes information from freight bills to a manifest which represents the shipment on a particular trailer. The billing clerk, as the name implies, prepares the bills which are sent to the customer. Then there are cashiers, payroll clerks, file clerks, accountants, typists and secretaries. Sales is another terminal function. Salesmen, many of whom started as freight handlers or clerks, call upon customers seeking their freight business for the trucking company.

There is a hierarchy of supervision in each terminal with a manager of customer service, accounting, sales and operations, all under a terminal manager, who invariably came up through the ranks. Above the terminal manager are management positions in the headquarters of the trucking firm.

This brief description of the on-the-job training available in truck terminals cannot convey that these are interesting jobs. Most terminals are amazingly busy places, handling a bewildering array of goods from many customers. Problems and crises are the rule. It is a busy, challenging, "never a dull moment" occupation.

America's inland waterways form a small but lively transportation industry. As you know, it is one of the oldest forms of transportation, which thrived through much of our nation's history. The Mississippi riverboat era of the mid-nineteenth century produced much romantic lore. Then riverboat commerce fell into decline with the coming of the railroads, only to begin a revival in the 1920s. Today there are 1,700 inland waterway operators doing business over 25,000 miles of inland waterways. They carry over 450 billion tons of freight with 3,900 towboats and tugboats and 16,000 barges. Much of the cargo is bulk commodities, for inland transport is by far the cheapest.

As in Mark Twain's day, life on the river is highly romantic, an existence full of sudden crises which tax the skills of the rivermen.

There are two methods of propulsion. Towboats are square on the bow and almost square at the stern, low in the water and quite squat-looking. Contrary to its name, the towboat pushes rather than pulls barges, perhaps as many as forty at a time. The tugboat had a shaped bow, sits higher in the water and has a rather racy look about it. It pulls barges astern on a hawser or pushes them by slipping its bow into a built-in slot in the stern of the barge. Generally speaking, towboats are used in calmer waters, tugboats in rougher waters.

There are 160,000 people employed on inland waterways. About half work on the boats and half on shore. The crew of a typical vessel might include a master pilot, a pilot, two engineers (either a chief engineer and an assistant or a first and second engineer), one mate, three deckhands and a cook.

A young man in this trade must grow up on the river. He begins as a deck-hand and becomes familiar with the waterway only through years of experience. He must learn the currents, shoals and sandbars. He must become familiar with the actions of the boats and tows in wind and wave, squall and calm, for piloting a tow over a river is an intricate business. The knowledge a master pilot possesses is largely pure instinct and a "feel" for his tow and the current. He cannot read it in a book or pass it on. A man must live it, progressing from deckhand to mate and then to pilot.

Hands may also become engineers by specializing as helpers and oilers to the engineer. It is preferred that the engineers pass the necessary tests to become licensed, but many do not.

The onshore jobs in inland waterways are similar to those just described for the trucking industry. Men and women handle cargo, maintain the boats, and perform billing, accounting and other terminal functions.

Chapter 11

Service Industries Offer Training

For many years high school graduates have become service workers, such as waiters, waitresses, cooks, bellhops, beauty operators, barbers, and many other occupations that involve serving customers, rather than making products or selling them. The lure of the service occupations has always been that little training is required. A young person could learn the skills on the job and often make a lot of money while doing it.

The service occupations offer greater opportunity today than ever before. As noted previously, ours is a service-oriented economy. Prolonged prosperity and personal affluence enables most Americans to enjoy service. We travel more, eat in restaurants, pay greater attention to our appearance, seek assistance in various ways—all of which has caused a demand for service workers.

"Service" has always been loosely defined. It is difficult to decide where service begins and ends. Salesmen believe they perform a service in that they help solve customer problems as well as selling them merchandise. The mechanic and repairman certainly perform a service. In this chapter the rather general interpretation of the word "service" will be extended, by including telephone operators. They certainly perform a service, but some group them under clerical employees.

About 250,000 operators are employed by America's telephone companies, yet there is a consistent shortage of qualified girls for this work. One might suppose that with the increased automation of telephone service—direct dialing of long-distance calls, for example—that the need for operators would diminish. But the reverse is true. Compare the number of operators today with the 115,000 employed as operators in 1920 before the introduction of the dial system in this country. The explanation lies solely in the growth of the telephone industry. There are so many more phones in use, and phone calls being made today than in the twenties. The peak employment of operators was in the 1950s prior to the introduction of direct dialing of long distance calls. Jobs began a gradual decline, then started going up again in 1963. Bell Systems executives anticipate increased employment in years ahead, because of the growing number of phone calls.

A career as a telephone operator offers several advantages to a girl. It is easily learned, far from strenuous and, despite its repetitive nature, rather fun. Dealing with the public is far from boring, for no two calls are alike. The operator encounters a cross-section of life, from frantic emergency calls to person-to-person calls to the President. Some operators keep a record of celebrities to whom they have talked on the phone or distant places they have contacted. Working conditions are usually ideal, and although an operator is sometimes too busy, there is time for friendships and ease.

Another great advantage to being a telephone operator is that it is a marketable skill. The experienced operator can find employment wherever she goes. Many women who have left work to rear families later return to work part time. Being an operator offers a woman a permanent marketable skill which seems likely to always be in demand.

Finally, as we shall see, there are excellent promotional opportunities for telephone operators. It offers a real career.

According to Peter B. Howell, traffic supervisor for American Telephone & Telegraph Company, high school graduates are preferred as telephone operators. You apply at a telephone company employment office. After filling out an application and being interviewed, you take tests which measure your mental ability and your aptitude for number transcription, spelling, filing and simple arithemetic. Telephone company employment officials check your high school performance, paying particular attention to your attendance record, for being regular about coming to work is important. At peak hours every operator is busy. If one is missing, telephone service deteriorates. Other factors personnel officers look for are a pleasing personality that will fit in well with the other operators and a pleasant voice. You should like people to be a good operator.

If you are hired, you will be assigned to a central office where an operator is needed. Usually you will go to work the next day. Your first day you will be assigned to a group chief operator, who will show you around, introduce you to the chief operator and explain the nature of your work.

Your formal training lasts two to three weeks. It is programmed training, so that you learn at your own speed. There are models of the switchboard equipment you will be using, but you will also receive training by handling actual calls at a regular switchboard. In your training you will learn to operate equipment, place calls, mark tickets and handle emergency calls. You usually begin with station-to-station calls, then progress to person-to-person calls and "coin calls" made from public booths.

There are several types of operators, but in all likelihood you will be trained either as a long-distance operator or as an information operator. The former is the familiar person who places person-to-person calls and assists with station-to-station calls. The information operator, again familiar, finds the numbers for customers. She uses a variety of directories, including biweekly and daily directories of new numbers, directories which list customers by address, the "yellow pages" and regular directories. Training for the information operator is similar to that for the long-distance operator, but usually somewhat shorter. Since the advent of direct long-distance dialing, telephone companies have experienced a large increase in the number of information calls.

Telephone operators have an eight-hour tour of duty, but since service must be provided around the clock, the operator's hours are most irregular. Every telephone company has peak hours, frequently from 9 to 11 in the morning, around 5 in the afternoon, and in the evening, when long distance rates become lower. Thus, the operators' hours are arranged to have the maximum number on duty at the peak hours. Some typical hours will be from 7:30 A.M. to 4:30 P.M.; 8 A.M. to 5 P.M.; 8:30 A.M. to 5:30 P.M.; 9 A.M. to 6 P.M. Then there are "split tours" from 8 A.M. to noon and 4 to 8 P.M. or 9 A.M. to noon and 6 to 10 P.M. Others have evening tours and a few night tours. Those working split tours and evening and night hours have shorter tours (4:30 to 10:30 P.M., for example) and receive higher pay. Part-time operators fit into this schedule with ease, perhaps working during peak afternoon or evening hours. Tours are chosen by seniority, so new operators should expect to receive the split tours or afternoon tours. New operators may also be assigned to the "relief trick," replacing operators on their days off. Her hours would be very irregular.

Operators have excellent promotional opportunities. The first step is to "service assistant," who supervises approximately twenty operators, aiding with problem calls and training new operators. Over her is the group chief operator, who is responsible for the training, attitude, service and safety of perhaps twenty-five or thirty operators. Responsible for the entire operations of the central office is the chief operator. Mr. Howell considers the chief operator a woman executive on the par with any in the country. She has total responsibility for all phases of management, including, in a large office, 150 to 200 operators. She may earn between $10,000 and $12,000 a year.

Bell Systems companies believe that to become a chief operator, a girl must be an operator first. Thus, promotion from the ranks is the rule. But so many girls are unwilling to assume the responsibility of such a position or devote the time such an executive position requires or lack the leadership ability that there is a shortage of what Mr. Howell calls "chief operator material." The young woman who would like to become a manager can find few better opportunities than the telephone industry.

The operator also has opportunities to move laterally into the commercial departments as a service representative, who handles subscriber problems and seeks ways to meet their service needs, and sales. Most importantly, the operator has learned a marketable skill. She can always find a job as an operator, and she will be in demand in business and industry as a switchboard operator.

The restaurant occupations have long been a major source of employment for individuals with a high school education or less. About 2.5 million are employed in approximately 350,000 public restaurants, cafeterias, snack bars, hamburger stands and other such places. Among the occupations are waiter and waitress; cook and chef; counter attendants, who serve food in cafeterias; busboys and busgirls, who clear tables and carry dishes back to the kitchen and sometimes set tables; kitchen workers, who wash dishes and prepare vegetables; pantry workers, who prepare salads and other dishes and janitors and porters.

With only a couple of notable exceptions, most of these jobs are easily learned and result in no particular skill. Depending on the type of restaurant in which one works, there are promotional opportunities to captain, headwaiter and various managerial positions, particularly in large restaurant chains.

The industry encompasses a broad range of opportunities. There are waiters and waitresses who earn the minimum wage (or less) and others who take home hundreds of dollars a week in tips. Waiters in top nightclubs and very plush restaurants make very substantial earnings. In practice the waiters are older men who have held their jobs for a long time. Such high-paying positions are difficult for the young person to obtain.

The highest-paying positions for women are as cocktail waitresses. Young, attractive girls are usually sought to wait on patrons in bars and lounges. Good figures are often demanded, particularly when the waitresses wear abbreviated costumes. Cocktail waitresses in busy places can earn as much as $200 or more a week in tips.

The major restaurant and hotel chains usually have enlightened personnel policies for waitresses, with training programs, regular shifts and various "fringe benefits."

The best opportunities to learn a marketable skill are in the kitchen trades. Skilled cooks and chiefs are highly sought after by restaurants and hotels. Cooking and baking is usually learned on the job. A young person starts as a kitchen helper, then progresses to pantryman or salad worker, gradually earning a promotion to third cook. He begins preparing simple foods under the guidance of the first cook or chef. Top chefs earn more than $20,000 a year.

At the other end of the scale are the dishwashers, porters and performers of other simple tasks. They need not be "dead end" jobs, but often are.

The restaurant industry expects continued growth in the years ahead, creating many new jobs. In addition, the industry has always had a high turnover rate in all but the top tip-earning positions. Many thousands of jobs will be available in the future.

Little need be said here about careers in the hotel industry. About 870,000 are employed in nearly 30,000 hotels and motels. There are three basic types of establishments: commercial hotels, which cater to transients; residential hotels and resorts, which serve vacationers. Hotels employ a wide variety of people—restaurant employees, bellhops, front-office clerks, room service attendants, chambermaids and porters. Many of these positions are tip-earning.

There are opportunities for training in the hotel field. A high school graduate starting as a room or desk clerk (who greets guests and assigns rooms), key clerks (who issue and receive room keys), reservation clerks (who acknowledge room reservations by mail or phone or teletype), rack clerks (who keep track of room occupancy) or mail and information clerks receive training which can lead to careers in hotel management.

A large hotel is a complex operation involving food service, room management, housekeeping, maintenance, bookkeeping and accounting, public relations and advertising, recreation and athletics, entertainment and tourist services. There are many opportunities for specialization leading to supervisory positions. There are hotel management courses in colleges, but the high school graduate can begin these careers with on-the-job training.

Those of you interested in becoming barbers or beauticians (also known as hairdressers and cosmetologists) must take formal courses for this, if only because practitioners are licensed by the state. To qualify for a license, a barber or beautician must pass a written test on the fundamentals of the trade and must demonstrate their skills.

There are hundreds of public and private barber colleges offering courses lasting from six to nine months. A student learns the basic services, such as haircutting, shaving, massaging and facial and scalp treatments. He works under supervision, practicing on fellow students and customers. There are formal classes and lectures in the use of barber implements, skin and scalp disorders and customer relations.

Nearly half the 180,000 barbers work in their own shops. Those who work for others receive a portion, generally about two-thirds, of the price charged each customer. Tips are an important source of earnings. The barber furnishes his own tools, which cost about $100.

Beauty operators can learn to cut, style, shampoo, set, straighten, bleach or tint hair (and manicure nails) in about 2,000 public and private schools, including vocational high schools. Courses last from six months to a year and include some classroom instruction and a great deal of practical experience on fellow students and customers. Graduates of such schools normally have no difficulty becoming licensed. With experience the beauty operator may specialize (advanced courses will help) in hair styling or coloring, permanent waving and other services.

Barbers are customarily (but not always) men. While the 485,000 beauty operators are predominantly women, there is a trend toward men entering this occupation.

The employment outlook for barbers and beauty operators is excellent, both from turnover and the growth in demand for these services.

There are a great many other types of service work for which a young person can qualify with little or no training. Among these are usher, bootblack, elevator operator, workers in laundries, dry-cleaning establishments, shoe repair places, travel agencies and many others. Job opportunities are often excellent, and most training is provided on the job. They do offer a chance to learn a marketable skill.

One of the largest categories of service worker is the gas station attendant, which again is learned by doing it. This has long been a popular source of both full time and part time employment for young men. The duties need little description. They include pumping gas, car washing, lubricating, changing tires and doing minor repairs on a car. Many thousands make a career of this occupation, going into station management and even ownership.

Chapter 12

Health Service Training

Some health service professions demand long and intensive training. Surgeons spend more than a decade attending university and medical school classes and as interns and residents in hospitals—a form of on-the-job training, although doctors hardly think of it in those terms. Dentists, podiatrists, chiropractors, veterinarians, dieticians and several other health service professions require training that goes far beyond high school.

Yet the field also includes a relatively larger number of people who perform important tasks with little or no training, such as nursing aides and orderlies. In between are health care occupations for which the high school graduate can qualify by training on the job and/or enrolling in certain courses.

The health service field now employs about 3.5 million men and women in hospitals, clinics, nursing homes, psychiatric institutions and offices of physicians and dentists. It is one of the fastest-growing areas of employment, with the nation both demanding and offering ever larger public and private health services. The Medicare program of the Federal Government has precipitated a significant extension of health care programs to the aged.

The expansion of health programs is causing a crisis in hospital administration. The costs of medical service are rising sharply, causing companion increases in hospital bills and health and casualty insurance premiums. At the same time, hospitals are endeavoring to cope with overcrowding, understaffing and outmoded buildings. Many hospital structures were built prior to the advent of modern medicine and cannot accommodate the new equipment being marketed today. All of these are problems which create both challenges and opportunities for the person entering the health service field today.

The quality of medical care is keeping pace with the quantity. Scientists are constantly pushing back the frontiers of medical knowledge with drugs, new surgical techniques and fresh understanding of fundamental body processes and their disorders. Hospitals today possess a vast array of equipment unknown a decade ago: heart, lung and kidney machines; automatic equipment to monitor pulse, respiration, temperature and other body functions and devices which analyze blood, urine and other body fluids and tissues. This mechanization creates opportunities for the electronic and mechanical technician. Increasingly, the operation of such equipment seems likely to be turned over to specially trained high school graduates.

No lessening is expected in the demand for nursing aides and orderlies. Men and women of high school education are recruited by the tens of thousands annually to assist nurses and doctors in caring for patients. Nursing aides and orderlies are important members of the health care team, performing indispensable services. A nursing aide changes beds, feeds patients, bathes them, measures temperature, pulse and respiration, comforts them and, to a large extent, enhances their mental health. More than any other member of the hospital staff, she observes the patient, talks to him and helps him remain cheerful and confident about getting well. These may be simple duties for which a person can be quickly trained, but they are important. The orderly does some or all of these duties, as well as assisting in moving patients to various parts of the hospital for therapeutic, laboratory and other services.

Training for aides and orderlies usually consists of a few class sessions at which techniques are described and demonstrated, plus on-the-job training under supervision.

Nursing aides are likely to remain aides unless they get some formal training. The easiest to accomplish is training to become a Licensed Practical Nurse (LPN). There are now about 370,000 LPNs who perform a variety of nursing tasks, including giving medications and simple treatments, as well as assisting in the care of patients. The number of LPNs is increasing rapidly, because usually only one year of training enables a person to pass the state licensing examination. Public schools now offer appropriate courses and some hospitals have gone over almost entirely to the training of LPNs.

Employment opportunities for LPNs are expected to remain excellent in the years ahead, for the LPN offers a compromise to a serious health problem, the chronic shortage of registered nurses. It takes a minimum of three years to train registered nurses, and the supply of RNs never seems equal to the demand. The LPN, while less trained and presumably less qualified to work with the seriously ill patient, has had sufficient training to meet the needs of the mildly ill or convalescing patient. Thus, hospitals, nursing homes and other medical institutions are seeking greater numbers of LPNs.

There is no way a girl can become an LPN with on-the-job training. She must take that year's training, but costs of training are quite low in many public hospitals. Many girls who begin as nursing aides could reasonably aspire to becoming LPNs.

A large step up the ladder is the RN. Nursing, with 700,-000 members, is the second largest profession for women next to teaching. There are several types of nurses, characterized by their places of employment. There are hospital nurses; private-duty nurses, who are employed directly by patients or their families; office nurses, who work for physicians in their offices or clinics; public health nurses, who work for government agencies and assist the indigent and elderly; and industrial nurses, who are employed in factory clinics and first aid centers. Hospital nurses compose about two-thirds of the total. Most are general nurses, but some specialize in obstetrics, pediatrics, surgery and other areas of medicine.

Nursing is a challenging profession with high standards and great responsibilities. The nurse gives medication, treats minor cuts and abrasions, changes surgical dressings, operates many types of modern medical equipment and performs scores of other treatments. She maintains direct care of the patient, carrying out the doctor's instructions.

To become a registered nurse takes a minimum of three years of training in a school of nursing operated by a hospital or university. Entrance requirements are a high school education with courses in chemistry and the biological sciences. Tuition is often minimal.

More young women are going into nursing today than ever before, yet the shortage of RNs continues, caused by the rising demand for health services and by the high turnover among nurses themselves. Marriage and motherhood annually remove a significant percentage of nurses from the profession. Thus, there is a great opportunity for the high school graduate who is not going on to college. The three years of training are mandatory, but easily financed by working for a year. Many scholarships and grants-in-aid are available.

There are other opportunities besides nursing. A high school graduate who has had courses in chemistry and biological sciences can find employment as an aide in a clinical or research laboratory in a university, hospital or other medical institution. The aide begins by doing simple tasks around the lab, such as washing implements, sterilizing, replenishing supplies, laying out equipment to be used in experiments. Eventually the aide is permitted to perform some simple tests and experimental procedures.

With proper training, the aide can become a fully qualified medical technologist. This is the person who performs laboratory tests to aid physicians in detecting, diagnosing and treating diseases. The technologist makes blood counts, skin tests, urinalyses; examines tissue microscopically; cultures bacteria and other organisms; determines blood types and blood coagulation and sedimentary rates and analyzes food, water and other materials for bacteria and impurities. He sometimes prepares slides (in detection of cancer, for example) and performs scores of other assignments under the direction of a physician, usually a pathologist. In small labs, the technologist performs a variety of tasks. In a larger lab, he may specialize in certain activities. Technologists work in hospitals, clinics, nursing homes, psychiatric institutions, drug manufacturing plants, police crime labs and university research institutions. Their skills are much in demand, and they do most interesting work, often participating in the great medical research of our times.

Most approved medical technology schools require three years of college training for entrance into courses which last fifteen to eighteen months. But this career has been included in this book because, like so many other occupations, the technologist is measured by what he or she can do, not by the length of education. A high school graduate, beginning as a laboratory aide, taking a few courses and applying himself can in the right setting learn the skills of the technologist, if not the formal title.

Another specialty to which the high school graduate can aspire is medical X-ray technician, who operates the X-ray equipment in medical institutions under the direction of physicians and radiologists. Most of you have seen an X-ray technician at work. He takes pictures of internal bones and organs, sometimes administering barium salts and other substances to make internal organs opaque. The technician positions the patient between the X-ray tube and the film. After determining the proper voltage, current and exposure time, the technician "snaps" the picture. The X-ray technique is also used for therapeutic treatment as with cancer.

To become an X-ray technician, you must enroll in a training program offered by a hospital or a medical school affiliated with a hospital. More than 700 such schools have been approved by the American Medical Association. The program usually lasts twenty-four months. A high school diploma is usually qualifying, although some college training is preferred.

No book of this kind can comprehensively report the full range or opportunities for training in modern hospitals. There is a fantastic array of equipment to be operated and maintained, and a shortage of people qualified for these jobs. The high school graduate who enters the health field as an aide or some form of assistant and shows ability, enthusiasm and willingness to learn will seldom have to wait long for an opportunity.

Dentistry also offers opportunities for young people. One career is dental hygienist, who, working under the supervision of a dentist, cleans teeth, massages gums and keeps records of patients' teeth. She may take and develop X rays, prepare materials to be used by the dentist, sterilize instruments and assist the dentist in his procedures. Hygienists are also employed by school systems to check and keep records of pupils' dental problems. They also work for public health agencies.

High school graduates can qualify for admission to a school accredited by the American Dental Association. The course lasts two years and leads to state certification as a dental hygienist. But there is an informal way to learn these skills. For decades dentists have trained their own assistants. It is certainly not the preferred way to train, but it is a place to begin and training can be augmented with formal courses. Again, it is ability and not the diploma that counts the most. Do not misconstrue this statement to mean that you are being encouraged not to enroll in accredited schools. On the contrary, you should if at all possible. All that is being said is that excellent hygienists have been trained by dentists in their offices.

First cousin to the dental hygienist is the dental laboratory technician, who works in laboratories and makes artificial dentures, crowns, bridges and other dental and orthodontal appliances. These items are ordered by the dentist, and the technician does not work directly with the patient. Artificial dentures are made from metal, porcelain, plastic and other substances. They conform precisely to plaster molds taken by the dentist. The technician uses a variety of tools, furnaces and other laboratory equipment in his work. He may specialize in certain kinds of dentures.

There are courses for training dental laboratory technicians offered in both public and private schools, but the most common way to enter the profession is as a trainee in a laboratory. Usually three to four years of on-the-job training are required to be fully qualified. The high school graduate with manual dexterity, good color perception and a pronounced sense of craftsmanship is sought as a trainee.

There are similar opportunities for training in eye care. A person may train to be an assistant to an optometrist or opthamologist, specializing in adjusting and fitting glasses. Optical mechanics are trained to grind and polish the lens which the "eye doctor" has ordered from a laboratory or has made in his own place of business.

Chapter 13

Government Training

All of the training opportunities discussed so far exist in a special, often advantageous way in federal, state and local government service. Because of these advantages, we should take a careful look at careers in government service. There is another reason for this chapter. Government is the largest and fastest growing employer in the United States. There are nearly 3 million people employed by the Federal Government, not counting the armed services. This is more than the next ten largest private employers combined. The state and local civil services dwarf even this figure, employing over 9,500,000. And employment by government, particularly state and local governments, is perhaps the fastest rising in the nation.

Government service is characterized by more than sheer numbers. Diversity is a rule. The Federal Government employs tens of thousands of scientists, engineers and technicians. There are more scientists than stenographers, more technicians than typists. The most advanced technology has a place in government. For example, the Federal Government is the largest single purchaser of computers. Cryogenists, cartographers, geodesists, entomologists, anthropologists, histologists, parasitologists and scores of other scientific specialists are employed in the Federal Service.

At the opposite end of the employment spectrum, there are busboys, waiters, warehouse workers, janitors, housekeepers and many other jobs for which an unskilled young person can qualify.

In between are hundreds of semiskilled and skilled positions. All of the building tradesmen and mechanical and electrical craftsmen are employed by government. Hundreds of thousands of secretaries, stenographers and other clerical employees work in government. There are nurses, X-ray technicians—all of the health service employees. In fact, just about every skill you can think of is used in government —and a few that are unique to government. Mail carriers and postal clerks are unique, as are several types of inspectors for regulatory agencies.

There are at least 1,500 different occupational specialties in the Federal Government. Some authorities have estimated that there may be as many as 15,000 actual job classifications. This array of skills needed by government creates excellent opportunities for the young person to receive training and career advancement.

In careers in government one does important, meaningful work. Government is connected in some way to nearly all aspects of our lives. For instance, government employees are helping to land men on the moon, studying the ocean's depths, seeking disease-resistant seeds for croplands, rehabilitating slums, ensuring that every American has the right to vote, purifying water supplies, building roads and helping to make the cars which run on them safer, teaching retarded children to read, seeking a cure for cancer, trying to guarantee peace and the brotherhood of man. When you work in government, you are a participant in the great events of our times.

This is true even if your job is simple. Delivering the mail is a relatively routine task performed by about 780,000 men and women. But it is vital work. Running a forklift in a military warehouse is essentially the same task as that performed in a private warehouse or terminal, but in government the forklift operator is contributing to national defense. The laboratory assistant in the National Institutes of Health is contributing in a meaningful way to a healthier America.

The importance of government work stems in part from its regulatory nature. A municipal health department insures that food is served in clean restaurants, that plumbing is sanitary, that food, water and drugs are correctly labeled. A building inspector supervises the work of contractors to see that legal standards for safety and workmanship are met. Just about every aspect of interstate commerce is regulated by government, and civil service employees enforce laws controlling dishonesty and discrimination.

A career in government, particularly the Federal Government, offers a high degree of flexibility. Under Federal Service rules, an employee has the right to unrestricted transfer. If he is a clerk in the Labor Department, for example, he can apply for a position as administrative assistant in the Commerce Department. If he is accepted, following an interview, he is encouraged to move to the higher-paying, more responsible position. And when he transfers he keeps all his retirement, vacations and other fringe benefits intact.

This policy of unlimited transfers is a great advantage to the young person. If he works for the Federal Government in virtually any capacity and desires to move into another line of work that has greater opportunity for training and advancement, he is free to do so. Such opportunities for transfer exist in some large corporations, but the sheer size and complexity of government service makes the opportunities for transfer much greater.

Government salaries are generally competitive with those in business and industry. The Federal Government especially has increased salaries to make them comparable to those "on the outside." At the middle and upper grades, the salaries frequently exceed those paid in private business.

At the same time, government service continues to offer a high degree of security. There are generous pension plans, sick-leave benefits, vacations and other fringe benefits. Government employees also have tenure. They cannot be fired without just cause, but there is always the risk that the job they perform may be eliminated, causing their unemployment. A generation ago the security aspects of government employment was its principal advantage. Government recruiters now downgrade this factor, emphasizing the meaningfulness, training and advancement opportunities and salary of civil service positions.

It would be a mistake to overstate the case for government employment. A differentiation must be made in the government one works for. The Federal Government has been progressive, especially since 1960, in upgrading its civil service. It raised salaries and standards. The policy of unlimited transfers was established. Recruiting campaigns were launched to attract the best young men and women to work at the federal level.

Not all of these progressive policies have been adopted at the state and local levels. A study of the New York City civil service, which is second in size to the Federal Service, shows that transfers cannot be made without the approval of a person's immediate superior. This makes transfers more difficult. A comparison of salaries paid in New York and in the Federal Service shows that higher wages are paid at the entry-level jobs in New York, but the middle and upper salaries are substantially lower. This is due in part to the fact that municipal services have greater need for people in the lower classifications, but the fact remains that the salary policies tend to reward the new, unskilled employee at the expense of the able, competent worker.

Politics is a greater hazard in local government than in the Federal Service. The situation is improving, but some local governments still exempt a large number of jobs from the civil service. Those who hold these positions may lose them when the opposite political party comes into power. The young person considering entering local government service ought to investigate to determine the political control which can be applied to his position.

Working for government is somewhat different from working for business and industry. There are more rules governing duties, training, promotions and salaries. The employee is classified according to the duties he performs and paid accordingly. Using the Federal Service as an example, all professional and scientific personnel (basically all but blue-collar workers) are classified on a scale from 1 to 18. A GS-1, as the classification is called, is a simple, unskilled position. A GS-18 is a highly skilled, professional supervisory position. Each classification has a salary rate, which rises as the employee spends more time in grade and gains more experience. Most jobs have a specified classification (sometimes more than one) and to advance to a high classification, the person must assume a new, more demanding position. To illustrate, stenographers are usually classified GS-3. If a particularly able stenographer is in a demanding job, she can be classified as GS-4 and, some-times, GS-5. If she wishes to advance to higher classifica-tions, she must become a secretary. She can then reach quite high classifications, depending upon the person to whom she is secretary. A cabinet officer might have a secre-tary ranking as a GS-11, while down the hall a junior executive might have only a GS-5 secretary.

The way to advance in classification is by training and experience—and by transferring to a position that offers a higher classification. In the Federal Service particularly, the classification rules are not overly rigid. A higher classifica-tion for the same job can be obtained. One of the most progressive federal policies is that which permits a profes-sional or skilled person to advance to quite high classifica-tions without taking on any supervisory duties. He may be doing individual research in a laboratory and advance to GS-15 simply because the work he is doing is important. This is not generally true in local service. As a rule, the employee must advance to supervisory positions in order to reach the higher classifications.

How do you get a government job? Again elaborate rules govern the process. You begin by taking a competitive examination. These are administered periodically, the frequency depending on the need for new employees. You go to a federal job application center to find out about open examinations, or to the personnel office of your state or local government.

The examination is given to all the applicants at one time (although not all examinations include a written test). The papers are graded and scored. When an opening is available, the top three or five scorers, depending on the civil service rules, are referred to the personnel officer of the government agency that has the opening. The agency selects that eligible person whom it feels is best qualified. Those eligibles who were not selected go back to the top of the list, subject to call at the next opening. The freedom to select also applies to the eligibles. If they do not want the job offered, they may refuse, go back on the list (usually called a register) and await another opening.

The competitive examination is appropriate to the job you are expected to do. A stenographer would be tested on her ability to type and take shorthand, spelling and other clerical knowledge. An electronics technician would be tested on his knowledge of that subject. In unskilled jobs the tests are quite simple.

Some positions are filled on the basis of experience and an interview, but these are usually unskilled positions, skilled craft jobs and special professional and scientific appointments.

The purpose of the competitive system and the other rules is to insure that the ablest and most qualified people obtain the available jobs. The system prohibits the political favoritism and nepotism which plagued government service for generations.

The result of the merit system and the upgrading of salary scales and promotional opportunities has been a distinct elevation of standards for government employment. All that has been written so far about the need for a marketable skill applies to government service. More and more, the best-qualified young people are seeking government careers, and government personnel officers find themselves with long lists of applicants from whom they can choose the most qualified. It is no longer easy to obtain a government job. For example, the Federal Government annually gives the

Federal Service Entrance Examination to many more college graduates than it ever hires. Governments have a plethora of applicants for the unskilled jobs, but, like business and industry, they are searching for technicians, craftsmen and clerical workers. They hire people with potential to learn, but there are many people who have this.

One of the reasons for the popularity of government service is that so much training is offered, particularly by the Federal Government. The types of training do not differ radically from that already described for business and industry, but the Federal Government, by the sheer size and complexity of its operations, has many well-established training procedures.

In my book, *Your Career in the Civil Service*, I told the story of Howard Larson, a native of Waukegan, Illinois, who graduated from Northwestern University. He took the Federal Service Entrance Examination and scored quite high. Several job offers came from various federal agencies, but he accepted a GS-5 post with the Fish and Wildlife Service of the Department of Interior at its National Fish Hatchery, Lake Mills, Wisconsin. He entered a training program where he was indoctrinated at three different hatcheries in one year. Then he was selected for a year's special training at Leetown, West Virginia. Next he was sent to graduate school at Auburn University and four months later went to Marion, Alabama, for a year's special training in warm water fish culture. Following a three year's assignment at La Crosse, Wisconsin, during which he rose to GS-12, he was sent to Washington, D. C., for an intensive course in government management. This is usually a prelude to further promotions. Of Mr. Larson's seven years in the federal service, half had been spent attending school.

Such a training record is perhaps not typical, but it indicates the extent to which the Federal Government will go to develop the potential of men it feels are particularly qualified.

On-the-job training is a way of life in government. An employee begins as an apprentice, helper or assistant and learns the skills by doing them and by working with experienced workers. This occurs in nearly all the blue-collar trades and crafts. Government hospitals are not essentially different from other public or nonprofit institutions, so the same opportunities for training in the nursing and health technology apply.

The Federal Service includes many categories of aides. Indeed, nearly every scientific and technical specialty has an aide associated with it. There are engineering aides, biological aides, laboratory, cartographic, electronic aides and many more. These are positions for which the inexperienced high school graduate can qualify. They offer opportunity to work in the scientific and technical fields and develop the skills which enable a person to become a technician.

In addition to on-the-job training, there are voluntary education programs. Government agencies regularly hold classes for their employees, teaching a wide range of subjects, liberal arts to specific skills. An unskilled clerical worker can enroll in typing or shorthand classes. A clerk can take accounting principles. An aide can enroll in courses in basic electronics. At the same time, workers are encouraged to enroll in night courses in colleges and technical schools.

Then, as we have seen, employees with potential and promise are enrolled in formal training programs to develop their skills and extend their knowledge. They are sent to universities, seminars and workshops of great variety.

There are new federal training programs which perhaps

go beyond what is being done by industry. The Civil Service Commission has instituted novel programs to enlarge the opportunities for minority groups and women to qualify for government employment.

The government's program to hire the so-called disadvantaged members of minority groups is one of high priority. One method being used in all federal agencies is to reappraise jobs so that the economically and educationally disadvantaged can qualify. This is the MUST program (Maximum Utilization of Skills and Training.) It aims to restructure existing jobs so that the less skilled tasks are separated from the skilled ones. Thus, a highly trained professional person may be doing simple, routine tasks which an unskilled person could perform. Under MUST, an unskilled person would be hired to do the routine assignments, leaving the professional employee to work at that for which he is best qualified. MUST carries a double benefit. The highest use is made of the skilled person, and a job is created for the unskilled.

The Civil Service Commission feels there is hardly a field in which this approach cannot be used. Dr. William H. Stewart, former surgeon general of the Public Health Service, spoke of the program's potential in these words: "Year by year, our top professional personnel are being trained to perform still more complex tasks. How long can each profession afford to hang on to its simple functions— the routine filling of a tooth, for example, or the several easily automated steps in a medical examination? How can we train the physician or dentist to make full use of the skills available to other people, freeing himself to perform only those duties for which he is uniquely qualified?"

The Public Health Service began hiring Indian nursing

assistants at GS-2 and GS-3 levels to work on Indian reservations under supervision of professional nurses. The assistants handle such tasks as skin tests for tuberculosis, certain home nursing assignments and assisting physicians in routine births.

The Social Security Administration set up a new GS-4 job for people to assist claims representatives. The new positions will be filled from a special examination which does not require a college background.

All possible effort and much innovation is being directed towards recruiting and training unskilled young people. One program seeks to enroll employees in adult-education programs set up in many communities under federal aid. These classes will teach such fundamental skills as reading, writing, speaking and arithmetic to former dropouts. Another program has established workshops to train supervisors of unskilled workers, particularly those from minority groups who have been unemployed for a long time. The supervisors are taught the needs of such workers, how to simplify the job assignments and how to motivate the employees. Another program aims to assist federal workers in obtaining high school equivalency certificates. High school dropouts who have attained knowledge and skills through on-the-job training are encouraged to take state exams to qualify for equivalency certificates. These can then be used in lieu of a high school diploma, thereby enabling a person to apply at technical schools and colleges which require a high school education for admittance.

These programs are being applied throughout the country on a regional basis. They have not yet been adopted by all of the state and local civil services, but the trend is clearly in this direction. In large cities, particularly, personnel departments are conscious of the need to employ and train unskilled young people, especially those from minority groups.

The future can only bring refinements of the training techniques. But there is a large application of the methods being forged at the federal level. Restructuring of jobs to separate the skilled from the less skilled tasks seems likely to have an ever widening application in business and industry, creating new opportunities for young people.

Chapter 14

Training in the
Protective Services

Throughout this book, every effort has been made to show that today's high school graduate is entering a rapidly changing world. As he or she seeks training and career advancement, one eye must always be cocked on the occupational horizon. How will the skill you are learning be changed a decade from now? Will it even exist? What must you do to prepare for the future?

Those of you who enter the scientific and technical fields must be particularly conscious of the future—and the future may be only tomorrow, so rapidly does the technology change. But, as we have seen, change is in the wind in every field of endeavor—retail sales, health care, government service, mechanical and repair work, traditional crafts. The production worker certainly has a greatly altered role.

In this chapter let's examine another career opportunity for the high school graduate which is changing rapidly. You might not think of the protective services as changing. Policemen, firemen and plant guards continue to look much the same as they have for generations. The goals of law enforcement, protection of individuals and property, are unaltered. But beneath the familiar facade a revolution is going on.

In part the revolution is technological. It began in the

1930s with the two-way police radio. This means of instant communication gave policemen far greater mobility. They could roam a city or a vast rural area in cars and remain in contact with their superiors. They could speed to the scene of a crime, call for medical aid or reinforcements, summon rescue vehicles. The coming of the radio was a tremendous advancement in law enforcement.

In the three decades that followed, other technological improvements were made with which you are familiar. Communications were futher developed with radar, teletype, walkie-talkies and portable public address systems. Crime laboratories were equipped with vapor fractometers, spectrographs, X-ray diffraction and many other devices for identifying minute specks of material. Police chemists became adept at blood sampling, narcotics recognition and analyses of minuscule portions of poisons, drugs and other chemicals.

But technological progress has only begun. The computer is just starting to be used in a few large police agencies, and its full potential has hardly been tapped. The computer will enable the police to keep up to the minute records on all crime and criminals. If detectives have a description of a bank robber, for example, the computer will produce in seconds a list of suspects fitting that description. The computer will categorize people by fingerprints, blood types, photographs, physical descriptions and other ways, then recall that information instantly. The computer will even be able to predict crime by analyzing the patterns of crime that have occurred. Police commanders will be able to deploy their men more effectively.

Since 1967 the Federal Bureau of Investigation has had in operation the National Crime Information Center (NCIC), a system that makes centralized computer information on wanted criminals and stolen items instantly available to police agencies all over the country. In 1971 a file of criminal histories was added to the NCIC system; this file makes criminal history data available to prosecutors, courts, and correction officers, as well as to law enforcement.

We are seeing only the beginning of the use of electronic devices in police work. Listening devices that can hear through the walls of a building or pick up a street-corner conversation from a block away will be in everyday use. A man will be recognized not just by his fingerprints or appearance, but by the sound of his voice accurately etched on paper for a permanent record. Tracer elements will be placed in narcotics and other commodities that are attractive to thieves which will permit positive identification of them. Automatic, infrared cameras will remove the sanctuary darkness has always afforded criminals. Electronic accounting procedures will certainly pose a far greater challenge to the embezzler and forger.

The point here is not that crime will disappear or that criminals will not be able to outwit the mechanical marvels. What is being said is that the coming of technology is creating a new type of policeman, trained in science and technology. He is being taught new skills that enable him to install, maintain and operate this new equipment and apply the information to the traditional tasks of law enforcement. The "cop on the beat" will know as much about electronics as he does guns.

That foot patrolman of the future will be operating in a very different manner. Chances are he won't be on foot at all. He'll be in cars equipped with a new array of devices, in motor scooters or helicopters. If he is on foot, he no longer will have to race to a call box to telephone the station house. He'll have a radio strapped to his belt.

It is inevitable that great mechanization and automation will occur in law enforcement. The rising volume of crime dictates that police agencies do everything possible to combat it. For the young person, these technological changes can be directly translated into training, specialization and career advancement.

There is a second aspect to the revolution in law enforcement. For the last decade, the United States Supreme Court has issued a series of historic opinions greatly extending the constitutional rights of accused persons and defendants and limiting the actions of police. A few illustrations: police cannot interrogate a suspect without first informing him of his right to remain silent and to call a lawyer; if the suspect asks to see a lawyer, one must be provided for him; police cannot conduct a search and seizure without a warrant, and a warrant cannot be issued without a really plausible reason; testimony by a witness at a legislative or other type of hearing cannot be used against him at a subsequent criminal trial; a defendant has the right to know the evidence to be brought against him; confessions obtained by surreptitious means cannot be used against an accused person; a suspect must be charged immediately and arraigned before a judge as soon as possible.

These decisions greatly extend the meaning of freedom in America. But they also pose serious problems for law enforcement, problems which are lending a new direction to police work. The court rulings are spurring the search for new mechanical and scientific means of obtaining evidence, so that the policeman's historic reliance on the confession can be discarded. The police are establishing interrogation centers where all questioning of a suspect is automatically recorded on sound film, which is sealed to prevent tampering. Special arrangements are being made for the immediate arraignment of charged persons.

For the young person entering law enforcement today all

of this means that he must be more highly trained in the law than he was formerly. In addition to his other duties, he will become much more legalistic. He will be more expert at gathering evidence. There will be more specialists in mechanical and laboratory phases of crime detection. In a word, he will need more brains, less brawn.

There is a third aspect to the revolution in law enforcement. More and more, the police officer is being asked to cope with the causes of crime and not just the criminals. The "men in blue" realize that crime is seeded in poverty, unemployment, poor housing, prejudice, inadequate education. Most police departments are already set up to deal with juvenile crime. A variety of special squads have been set up to assist youngsters who break the law. The trend today is toward educating young people in traffic safety, rather than simply arresting speeders; to rehabilitating alcoholics, rather than just throwing drunks into jail; to seeking treatment for drug addicts rather than simply bringing charges against them. The modern police officer is becoming indoctrinated in the social forces of urban ghettos which breed crime, and he is being trained to enforce the law with sensitivity, particularly in matters that have racial overtones.

The need to be a social worker as well as a "cop" has meant a difficult adjustment for many older policemen. But the tone of court decisions is in this direction. The trend in law enforcement is clearly toward more humanity. This means the police officer of the future will be better informed about public affairs and more aware of how his conduct can affect them.

These three factors do indeed compose a revolution. The police department of the future will be more professional than many are today. It has been traditional in police work that the only qualifications a man needed to be promoted was to have been a "good cop"—that is, he had performed his duties well, had developed a good record for arresting offenders and had been commended for meritorious service or valor. Our best police departments realize today that more than this is needed. To become a high-ranking officer, an individual needs to know public administration, budgeting and finance and proper personnel practices. He should be an expert in modern police methods, such as deployment of patrol forces, communication and crime detection. He should be aware of the social forces that cause crime and the role police can play in ameliorating them. He should have a well-developed sense of public relations—that is, he should be conscious of public attitudes towards the police department and what the police can do to foster public confidence. All of this is a large order, but clearly the future points in this direction.

Any discussion of present police training programs must point out that the revolution of which we are speaking is just beginning. Neither the status of police officers nor the salaries they earn has enabled departments to recruit men of the caliber they need. In only a handful of communities have the training methods been altered to teach men (and women) the methods they will be using in the future. Again the trend is toward better training. The International Association of Chiefs of Police has been conducting a program for years to upgrade the caliber of men recruited and their training. The IACP has endeavored to instill in senior officers a need for more efficient and modern methods of crime prevention and detection—and with good effect. The Federal Government has established a commission to improve police training at local levels. The Federal Bureau of Investigation has for years opened its academy to local police officers. These men return to indoctrinate others with the progressive practices.

Yet the fact remains that these efforts are not enough. One city of over 500,000 population provides its patrolmen with only one week of training. Only a few departments have established any comprehensive program for retraining men who have been promoted to higher ranks. But all of this is changing. A young man entering law enforcement today will be asked to amalgamate the best of the old methods with experimental new ones. He will be taught a variety of electronic and mechanical skills. If he shows promise, he may spend as much time in the classroom as on the beat, at least in his early years.

One of the finest police academies in the country is that operated by the New York City Police Department. The recruit trains from 9 A.M. to 5 P.M. with about half this time spent in academic classes, the remainder in physical and firearms training. He is organized into military type companies under command of an instructor.

In the classroom he learns about ethics and conduct, his equipment, organization of the department, and reports, records and orders. He learns how to conduct himself as a policeman, courtesy, the nature of police discipline, including charges that can be brought against him for wrongdoing and awards and commendations he can receive for superior work. He is taught first aid, what to do if a person is dead, how to cope with deranged individuals, and how to care for the lost, destitute or neglected. He learns how to investigate all types of accidents. The curriculum includes all facets of police patrolling: how to preserve the peace, his duties when on motorized patrol, how to describe people and property and turn in alarms, and the actions he should take when he encounters various types of crime. He is taught the various traffic regulations and how to cope with traffic problems. Learning how to receive, record and refer complaints, how to make arrests and how to conduct searches and seizures is an important part of his studies. Then he becomes an expert in criminal law, learning what the laws are and what constitutes a violation of them—and there are hundreds of laws, from simple assault to murder, from purse snatching to bank robbery, which he must know. Finally, he learns not just what is expected of him, but what he should expect from lawbreakers and the general public. This list, and it is far from a complete one, is intended to indicate that a policeman has a great deal to learn.

In his firearms training he becomes most expert in handling various weapons safely, while elevating his marksmanship to a high level. In physical fitness classes he toughens his body and learns to use the nightstick and handcuffs and how to search and frisk suspects. In boxing and judo classes he learns the art of self-defense. His eighty-one days of training are certainly busy ones.

But the officer's training never stops. No two days in a policeman's life are ever the same. He is always encountering new situations to test his knowledge and ability.

There are many opportunities for specialization. He can go into communications, learning radio techniques and teletype procedures. Many police officers become expert in communications. The crime lab trains men who have a background in chemistry and physics to be lab technicians. The detective is another specialist, as are members of the rescue squad, riot squad, youth squad and narcotics bureau. The person with a love for animals can find a home in the mounted unit or the canine patrol force.

Opportunities for training in police work are not limited to uniformed members. Police departments employ large numbers of civilians, whom they train for auxiliary functions. Again there is a trend towards turning as many routine functions as possible over to civilians, freeing police officers for the duties they were trained to do. Law enforcement agencies at the federal, state and local levels employ and train clerks and other clerical personnel, telephone operators, radio operators, mechanics, photographers, lab technicians, and a variety of radio, electronics and other types of repairmen. The FBI trains fingerprint clerks. The FBI, as you know, is the national depository for fingerprint records, and it receives hundreds of requests daily to identify fingerprints, as well as similar requests to identify forged signatures and check papers, inks and other substances. Some of these identification tasks are performed by clerks trained by the FBI.

The term "protective service" means more than law enforcement. It encompasses plant protective forces, and large industrial plants often have quite large security forces. Guards are employed, either by individual businesses or by detective agencies who provide the service to many firms. They patrol warehouses, stores, recreation facilities and other types of public property. Many former police officers go into this type of work, but large firms and detective agencies train their own men.

Firemen also receive extensive training. Through formal study and practice drills at the fire service school operated by the local fire department, the recruits learn about local building codes, fire prevention, ventilation, first aid and the use of lifelines, chemical extinguishers, ladders and other fire fighting equipment. Their training continues on the job at the fire companies to which they are assigned.

Careers in law enforcement, plant protection and fire service have long been attractive to high school graduates. Most departments require a high school diploma or equivalent, although some agencies have lowered their standards. The applicant should be twenty-one years old and in excellent health. There are usually height and weight limitations.

The FBI and United States Treasury Agents must meet

much higher standards. In the latter service a college education is minimal, while the FBI requires that an agent have a law degree, be an accountant or have a 4-year degree in a field for which the FBI has a need. These standards do not apply to civilian employees. A college degree is not required to be a United States Postal Inspector, but the applicant is expected to be a Post Office employee.

Chapter 15

A Word to the College Bound

With more than half of the high school graduates attending college, some alteration in the traditional role of the college educated seems inevitable. Historically, the college graduates were leaders. They became professional men and women, scientists, executives in business and industry, artists and musicians.

These roles will remain unchanged for a substantial portion of the college graduates, but it seems unlikely that in the future all college-educated persons can be so employed. If they were, we would become a nation with more chiefs than Indians.

No particular sagacity is required to visualize that in the future, college graduates will be performing tasks now done by high school graduates. There is some overlapping already. Technicians can be either college trained or high school graduates. Skilled clerical workers are largely high school graduates, but many have college diplomas. A mixture is found in sales, health service and certain other occupations. There appears to be a trend toward this.

During interviews with personnel officers in preparation of this book, some discussion was held about the future role of the college trained. Out of these discussions came a piece of advice: not all, certainly, but some college-bound youngsters would be quite smart if they would overtrain for a job.

A few illustrations might help to explain. As has been noted, telephone companies have a difficult time finding chief operators. To relieve the shortage, phone company executives are already endeavoring to recruit college graduates to become telephone operators. The recruiters believe that if the college girl realizes the advancement opportunities, she will be willing to start at the bottom as an operator.

Another example: would an engineer be smart to take a production job in a factory? Indeed he would. Personnel officers at IBM's East Fishkill components factory said they had never heard of an engineer doing such a thing, but admitted it might be a wise move. The normal progression for a production worker is to technician and then to department manager. An engineer in production would have such an immense advantage over his less-skilled co-workers that he would be taking the quick road into management—as well as learning the business from the bottom up.

This overtraining technique could be used in any manufacturing industry. It would also work in sales. Supermarkets admit to having trouble recruiting college graduates simply because they are expected to stack cans and do other clerking tasks for at least a while. A college graduate who starts as a night clerk in a hotel, an appliance serviceman, a freight handler in a truck terminal, a reservations agent in an airline office or a score of similar capacities would be taking a big career shortcut, for he would be playing the role of a big frog in a little pond.

All the personnel officers who discussed these ideas admitted the scheme opposes human nature. The college grad wants to lead, not start at the bottom. He wants to use his knowledge, not learn skills to enhance his knowledge. But human nature can change, and as college enrollments increase, it may have to.

But whether you go to college or take a job after high school, some splendid training opportunities await you. Good luck! Much success!

Index

ABOUT THE AUTHOR

Robert A. Liston was born and brought up in Ohio and attended Hiram College in that state, majoring in history and political science. After college he went to New York, married and worked at a variety of jobs that took him into Iowa, Texas and California. He entered the Army during the Korean conflict and edited a frontline newspaper with the 45th Division. He was a working journalist from 1954 to 1964 and then turned to free lance writing, and has more than a score of books for young adults to his credit.

The Listons and their three children spent several years living in a lovely villa overlooking the Mediterranean on Spain's Costa del Sol and have recently returned to the United States. When Bob is not writing, he and his family are traveling.